Name _____ Date _____

Uses of Numbers

Look at the cartoons. Read the sentences.

Fill each blank with a word from the box.

| show position | count | measure | label |

1. My brother is 3 feet tall. I am using numbers to ___measure___.

2. This is Classroom 11. Welcome! I am using numbers to ___label___.

3. Your seat is in the 8th row. I am using numbers to ___show position___.

4. I need 24 pens for my class. I am using numbers to ___count___.

Copyright © Houghton Mifflin Company. All rights reserved.

Use with text pages 4–5.

D1379081

Name _____ Date _____

Place Value Through Hundred Thousands

Read the definitions.

To **increase** means "to make larger." The balloon is **increasing** in size.

25¢   10¢

Greater can mean "more" or "larger." A quarter has **greater** value than a dime.

To **decrease** means "to make smaller." The snowman is **decreasing** in size.

50¢   5¢

Ten times greater means "a value multiplied by 10." A fifty-cent piece has a value **ten times greater** than a nickel.

Write *increasing* or *decreasing* below each picture.

1.

decreasing
_____

2.

increasing
_____

3. Circle the stamp with the *greater* value.

4. Circle the piece of money that has a value *ten times greater than* a dime.

1¢   25¢

$1.00

Copyright © Houghton Mifflin Company. All rights reserved.

Use with text pages 6–8.

Problem-Solving Strategy:
Use Logical Reasoning

Read each problem. Fill in the blanks.

BANANA

LEMON

1. Liza and Kit each have a piece of fruit. No one has a fruit that begins with the first letter of her name.

   So, Liza has a _____ banana _____. Kit has a _____ lemon _____.

2. Ben and Luke each have a blue or a red flower. Ben's flower is not red.

   So, Ben's flower is _____ blue _____. Luke's flower is _____ red _____.

3. Bela and Anton each own a van or a motorcycle. Bela does not own a vehicle with two wheels.

   So, Anton owns a _____ motorcycle _____. Bela owns a _____ van _____.

4. Marta and Cia are the only people standing in line. Marta is not last.

   So, _____ Marta _____ is in front of _____ Cia _____.

5. Lori and Pam are playing a game. One of them has scored 18 points. The other has scored 13 points. Pam does not have more points than Lori.

   So, Pam has _____ 13 _____ points. Lori has _____ 18 _____ points.

Copyright © Houghton Mifflin Company. All rights reserved.

Use with text pages 10–13.

Name _____ Date _____

How Big Is One Million?

Read the comic strip. Think about the words in bold type.

1.

P: Darren, this book is fun! It has 8 pages of jokes and 4 pages of puzzles.

D: So, it has 12 pages **altogether**.

2.

D: Paul, you have done 3 of the 4 pages of puzzles.

P: Yes, there is 1 **remaining** puzzle page.

3.

D: Have you seen this joke book? I read it **cover to cover** last night.

P: Wow, you read every page!

4.

P: I have an idea! Let's **combine** our favorite jokes into a super joke book!

D: Let's do it! It will be fun to put our jokes together.

Draw lines to connect the words to their meanings.

1. cover to cover   "as a total number"

2. altogether   "put together"

3. remaining   "every page"

4. combine   "not used yet, or still there"

Use the words in the box to complete the sentences below.

cover to cover	altogether	remaining	combine

5. You can _____ red paint and yellow paint to make orange paint.

6. If you have used 4 of 6 paper cups, you have 2 _____.

7. If you have 2 red pens and 3 blue pens, you have 5 pens _____.

8. When you have read all of a book, you have read it _____.

Copyright © Houghton Mifflin Company. All rights reserved.

Use with text pages 14–15.

Place Value Through Hundred Millions

Standard form is the usual way in which numbers are written. The number in the box is written in standard form: 5,280

Expanded form is a way of writing a number to show the values of its digits. The number in the oval is written in expanded form:
5,000 + 200 + 80

Short word form is a way of writing a number with words and digits. The number on the dotted line is written in short word form:
5 thousand, 280

Word form is writing a number in words. The number in the cloud is written in word form:

five thousand, two hundred eighty

Connect the numbers to the forms they are in.

1. one thousand, seven hundred sixty   standard form

2. 1,760   expanded form

3. 1 thousand, 760   short word form

4. 1000 + 700 + 60   word form

Complete these items.

5. Write a digit in each box: ☐☐☐☐☐

5–9: Answers will vary.

6. Write the digits above as a number that is in standard form. _____

7. Write the number above in expanded form. _____

8. Write the number above in short word form.

_____

9. Write the number above in word form.

_____

Copyright © Houghton Mifflin Company. All rights reserved.

Use with text pages 16–18.

Compare Numbers

Look at the pictures. Read the phrases.

ride horseback

see gems and minerals on display

go bicycle riding

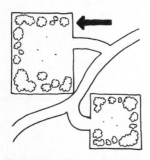

the greater number of acres

go mountain climbing

rent a bicycle

Find a phrase above that means the same as the phrase below. Write the phrase on the blank.

1. climb to the top of a mountain _____

2. ride on a horse _____

3. pay to use a bicycle for a while _____

4. more acres than another place has _____

5. look at a display of beautiful, valuable rocks _____

6. ride on a bicycle _____

Copyright © Houghton Mifflin Company. All rights reserved.

Use with text pages 24–25.

Name _____   Date _____

Order Numbers

Read the information in this chart.

One Way to Say It	Another Way to Say It	Example
from least to greatest	from smallest to largest	$1 < 4 < 12$
from greatest to least	from largest to smallest	$12 > 4 > 1$
the greatest place	the place with the largest value	⑦0 9 1
the greatest digit	the largest number in a certain place	7⑧2 7 5 6 7 2 6
the least number	the number with the fewest digits; the smallest number	128 ㊸ 4951
the greatest number	the number with the most digits; the largest number	128 43 ④951

Underline the phrase that fits each example.

1. $7 < 10 < 17$ <u>from least to greatest</u>   from greatest to least

2. $22 > 21 > 20$ from least to greatest   <u>from greatest to least</u>

3. ⑥ 9 5   the greatest digit   <u>the greatest place</u>

4. 5 1 5   <u>the greatest digit</u>   the greatest place
   5 2 5
   5 ⑥ 0

5. 6   ⑯④   98   the least number   <u>the greatest number</u>

6. ⑥   164   98   <u>the least number</u>   the greatest number

Copyright © Houghton Mifflin Company. All rights reserved.   **Use with text pages 26–28.**

Name _____ Date _____

Compare and Order Money

Read the explanations.

> **Greater** and **greatest** are forms of the word **great**. In math,
> **greater** means "more" or "larger." **Greatest** means "the most"
> or "the largest."
>
> **Less, lesser,** and **least** are forms of the word **little**. In math, **less**
> means "not as many" or "not as much." **Lesser** means "smaller."
> **Least** means "the smallest" or "the smallest amount."

Draw a line under the correct form.

1. A five-dollar bill has (greater, greatest) value than a one-dollar bill.

2. 999 is the (greater, greatest) three-digit number.

3. 25¢ is (less, least) than 50¢.

4. The U.S. coin with the (less, least) value is the penny.

5. $2.50 is a (lesser, least) amount than $2.75.

Complete each sentence. Write *greater* or *less*.

6. 51 is ____less____ than 55.

7. $30.00 is ___greater___ than $20.00.

8. The number of days in a month is ____less____ than the number of days in a year.

9. The number of days in a month is ___greater___ than the number of days in a week.

Complete each sentence. Write *greater* or *lesser*.

10. A quarter has ___greater___ value than a dime.

11. If you lose a penny, you have a ___lesser___ number of coins.

Complete each sentence. Write *greatest* or *least*.

12. The ___least___ number of days a year can have is 365.

13. The ___greatest___ number of days a year can have is 366.

14. The bill with the ___least___ value is the one-dollar bill.

Copyright © Houghton Mifflin Company. All rights reserved.

Use with text pages 30–32.

Make Change

Read this explanation.

> The word **change** often means "to become different."
> When **change** is used to talk about money, it means
> one of these things:
>
> - "the amount of money you get back when you give a clerk
>   more money than the cost of what you are buying"
>
>   *Example:* If you are buying something that costs $4.50 and
>   you give a clerk a five-dollar bill, the clerk will give you fifty
>   cents in **change**.
>
> - "some coins"
>
>   *Example:* Many people keep **change** in their car to use in
>   parking meters.

**Draw lines to connect the meanings with the
way *change* is used in each sentence.**

1. Sheila carries **change** in a
   small red coin purse.

2. When a person gives Sam a
   twenty-dollar bill to pay for a quart
   of milk, he must make **change.**

3. The new coat of paint made a
   big **change** in the appearance
   of the school.

4. The leaves of the trees **change**
   color in the fall.

"to become different"

"a difference"

"money you get back
from a clerk"

"some coins"

**Fill in the blanks so the sentence tells about something
you bought.** Answers will vary.

5. I bought a _____. The price was _____. I gave the clerk

   _____. The clerk gave me back _____ in change.

Copyright © Houghton Mifflin Company. All rights reserved.

Use with text pages 34–36.

Round Numbers

Read this explanation.

A circle is a **round** shape. ○

A zero looks like a circle. 0

A **round** number is a number that ends with one or more zeros.
Here are some round numbers: 100   3,500   200,000

When you **round** a number, you change it from an exact number
to a number that ends with one or more zeros. This process is
called **rounding.**

When you round a number to the **nearest ten,** you round it to
the nearest number with at least one zero. When you round a
number to the **nearest hundred,** you round it to the nearest
number with two or more zeros. When you round a number to
the **nearest thousand,** you round it to the nearest number with
three or more zeros.

Complete each item below.

1. Circle the round shapes.

2. Circle the round numbers.

4200   6757   10,000,000   705   125,000

3. Circle the box with a number that has been rounded.

2156 → 2200   2156 → 215   2156 → 2 + 1 + 5 + 6

4. Circle the box with a number that has been rounded to the nearest hundred.

836 → 840   836 → 800   836 → 1000

5. Circle the box with a number that has been rounded to the nearest thousand.

836 → 840   836 → 800   836 → 1000

Copyright © Houghton Mifflin Company. All rights reserved.

Use with text pages 38–39.

Problem-Solving Application:
Use a Bar Graph

Read this explanation.

A noun is a word that names a person, place, thing, or idea. In
English, one noun can be used with another noun to name something.
The first noun often tells "what kind" about the second noun.

Read these phrases. They are each made up of nouns.
The pictures show the things they name.

community center

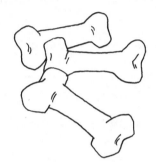

dog bones

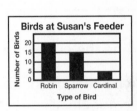

bar graph

theme park

hockey team

race car track

Use the phrases from above to complete these sentences.

1. If you want to see cars go fast, you should go to a _____.

2. A graph in which bars show amounts is a _____.

3. You can make a puppy happy by giving it _____ to chew on.

4. If you want to play basketball or do some other activity, you can go
   to a _____.

5. You must be able to skate on ice to play on a _____.

6. If you want to ride a roller coaster, you should go to a _____.

Copyright © Houghton Mifflin Company. All rights reserved.

Use with text pages 40–42.

Name _____ Date _____

Learners
3.1

Addition Properties and Subtraction Rules

Read this explanation.

Commute can mean "to exchange."

The **Commutative Property** has to do with exchanging, or changing, the order of numbers you are adding.

Associate means "to group together" or "to join in a relationship."

The **Associative Property** has to do with how you group the numbers you are adding.

Underline the correct terms in parentheses.

1. If you change the order of two numbers you are adding, you (commute, associate) the numbers.

2. If you change the way you group the numbers you are adding, you (commute, associate) the numbers in a new way.

3. If you change 17 + 200 to 200 + 17, you are using the (commutative, associative) property.

4. If you regroup (5 + 2) + 8 as 5 + (2 + 8), you are using the (commutative, associative) property.

5. If you leave one group and join another, you (commute, associate) with new people.

6. Going somewhere to work and then back home every day is called (commuting, associating).

7. People who join together for a purpose may call themselves (a commutation, an association).

Copyright © Houghton Mifflin Company. All rights reserved.

Use with text pages 60–61.

Name _____ Date _____

Mental Math Strategies

Read these definitions.

break apart	to separate
compensate	to make up for a loss
trade	to give something in exchange for something else
collect	to gather together in a group
remove	to take off

Use words from the box to complete the sentences.

broke apart	compensated	traded	collected	removed

1. Val _____ a red pen to Fumi for a brush. traded

2. Ernesto _____ a rock from his shoe. removed

3. The little shed _____ in the storm. broke apart

4. When the cleaners ruined Alicia's dress, they _____ her by giving her twenty dollars. compensated

5. Al and his brother Farid _____ shells at the beach last week. collected

Copyright © Houghton Mifflin Company. All rights reserved.

Use with text pages 62–63.

Estimate Sums and Differences

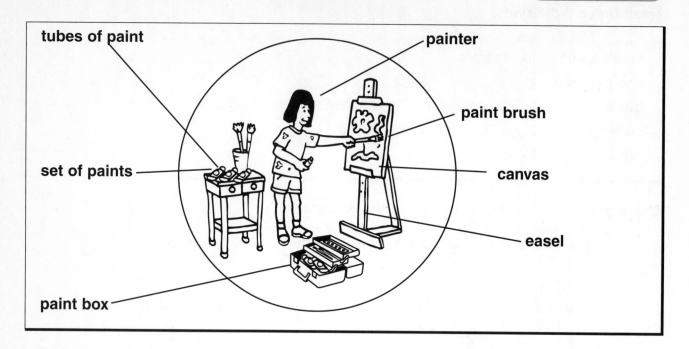

tubes of paint

painter

paint brush

set of paints

canvas

easel

paint box

Fill each blank with a word from the box.

paints	box	easel	tubes	canvas	brush

1. The painter chooses a _canvas_ to paint a picture on.

2. She sets it on an _easel_ so she can paint on it standing up.

3. She opens her paint _box_ and checks the colors in it.

4. She keeps _tubes_ of paint on a table, in case she needs them.

5. She also keeps a set of _paints_ on the table.

6. Then she picks up a _brush_ and begins to paint with it.

Copyright © Houghton Mifflin Company. All rights reserved.

Use with text pages 64–67.

Problem-Solving Decision:
Estimate or Exact Answer

Read this information.

Sometimes you need to know **exactly** how many.

Example: You are asked how many more lunches were served today than were served yesterday. You need to find the **exact amount**.

Sometimes you just need to find out about how many.

Example: You are asked **about** how many students are in your school. You can **estimate** the sum.

Read each item carefully. Decide whether you would need an exact answer or an estimate. Circle your choice.

1. Ned is planning a meeting. He needs to know how many students will come.

   (exact answer)   estimate

2. Val needs to find out about how many photographs will fit in a photo album.

   exact answer   (estimate)

3. Shelly is planning a picnic. She needs to know about how many olives people will eat.

   exact answer   (estimate)

4. Tom needs to figure out whether he has spent more than $25 on food for the picnic.

   (exact answer)   estimate

5. Julio needs to know how many seats there are in the two buses that will take students to the picnic.

   (exact answer)   estimate

Copyright © Houghton Mifflin Company. All rights reserved.

Use with text page 68.

Add Whole Numbers

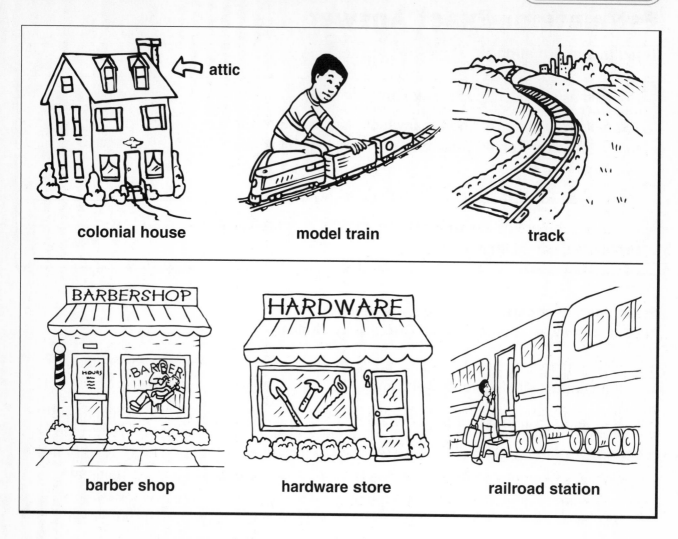

colonial house   model train   track

barber shop   hardware store   railroad station

Look at the pictures and the words in bold type.
Write words in bold type to solve the riddles.

1. I am a place where you can get a haircut. _____ barber shop

2. I am a toy that goes along a track. _____ model train

3. I am a kind of home. _____ colonial house

4. I am a store where you can buy tools. _____ hardware store

5. I am the place you go to get on a train. _____ railroad station

6. I am a room at the top of a tall house. _____ attic

7. I am a path for a train. _____ track

Copyright © Houghton Mifflin Company. All rights reserved.

Use with text pages 70–71.

Subtract Whole Numbers

Read the terms and definitions.

set up	to put things in place so you can do something
line up	to move into a straight row
knock down	to use force to make something fall to the ground
regroup	to put together in a new way
undo	to reverse or take apart
complete	to finish

Underline the correct terms in parentheses.

Rory and Zoila are going to play with dominos. Rory will (set up, undo) some dominos in a circle. Then Rory will (complete, knock down) a domino. That domino will (regroup, knock down) another domino, and so on. Soon all the dominos will be flat on the floor. After that, Rory and Zoila will (complete, regroup) the dominos. Rory will (undo, set up) one group of dominos in the shape of the letter I. Zoila will (knock down, line up) the other group of dominos in two rows. Then the two children will (undo, regroup) all their work. Each of them will give one domino a push. Those dominos will (regroup, knock down) two others. In a few seconds all the dominos will be flat on the floor once again. When Zoila and Rory (complete, set up) this game, they will put all the dominos back in the box.

Write a sentence about something you have set up.

Answers will vary.
_____

Write a sentence about something you have knocked down.

Answers will vary.
_____

Copyright © Houghton Mifflin Company. All rights reserved.

Use with text pages 72–73.

Subtract Across Zeros

Look at the drawings. Read the sentences.

 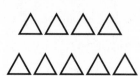 

I thought there were 7 triangles.

There are actually 9 triangles.

That is 2 more than I thought there were.

Look at the cartoons. Write numbers to make the sentences tell about the cartoons.

1. I thought there were ___5___ eggs on the stand.

2. There are actually ___12___ eggs.

3. That is ___7___ more than I thought there were.

Look at the drawings. Write sentences that tell about them.

4. I thought there were 4 triangles. _____

5. There are actually 6 triangles. _____

6. That is 2 more than I thought there were. _____

Copyright © Houghton Mifflin Company. All rights reserved.

Use with text pages 74–75.

Name _____ Date _____

Add and Subtract Greater Numbers

Read the explanations.

An **ear of corn** is the part of the corn plant that people eat.

A **mural** is a big work of art on a wall.

A **panel** is one part of something flat. It is usually a rectangle.

A **palace** is a big, fancy building.

A **bird feeder** has seeds or other food that birds like to eat.

Draw lines to the correct answers.

1. Which is a **palace**?

2. Which is an **ear of corn**?

3. Which is a **mural**?

4. Which is a **bird feeder**?

Circle any panel.

5.

Students may circle any of the panels.

Fill in the blanks with words from the box. Make the sentences tell about the picture.

ears of corn	mural	bird feeder

6. This big work of art is a __mural__.

7. It is being made out of __ears of corn__.

8. Birds love corn, so this work of art can become

   a __bird feeder__ later.

Copyright © Houghton Mifflin Company. All rights reserved.

Use with text pages 76–78.

Name _____ Date _____

Multiplication Properties and Division Rules

Read these explanations.

Commute can mean "to exchange." The **commutative property** has to do with exchanging, or changing, the order of numbers you are multiplying.

Associate means "to group together" or "to join in a relationship." The **associative property** has to do with how you group the numbers you are multiplying.

The **property of one** is a rule about multiplying by the number 1.

The **zero property** is a rule about multiplying by the number 0.

Underline the correct terms in parentheses.

1. If you change the way you group the numbers you are multiplying, you (commute, associate) the numbers in a new way.

2. If you change the order of two numbers you are multiplying, you (commute, associate) the numbers.

3. If you change 4×3 to 3×4, you are using the (commutative, associative) property.

4. If you regroup $(5 \times 2) \times 3$ as $5 \times (2 \times 3)$, you are using the (commutative, associative) property.

5. The property of (one, zero) can help you figure out the answer to 777×1.

6. The (one, zero) property can help you figure out the answer to 609×0.

Copyright © Houghton Mifflin Company. All rights reserved.

Use with text pages 84–86.

Relate Multiplication and Division

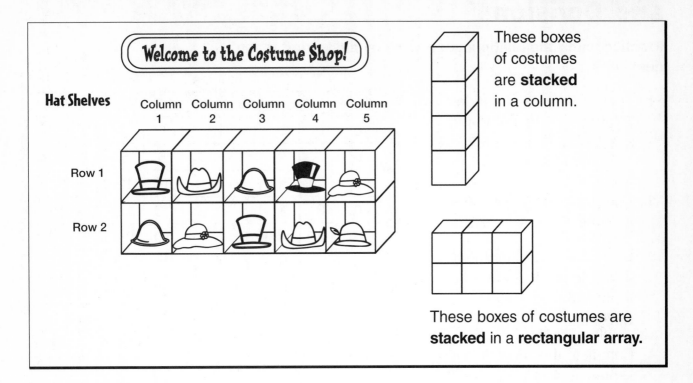

Welcome to the Costume Shop!

Hat Shelves

| | Column 1 | Column 2 | Column 3 | Column 4 | Column 5 |

Row 1

Row 2

These boxes of costumes are **stacked** in a column.

These boxes of costumes are **stacked** in a **rectangular array.**

Look at the drawing. Then answer the questions.

1. Which go up-and-down, rows or columns? __columns__

2. How many hats are stored in each column? __2__

3. How many hats are stored in each row? __5__

4. How many hats are stored in all? __10__

5. If you **stack** things, do you make a column or a row? __You make a column.__

6. How many columns are in the rectangular array of boxes? __3__

7. How many rows are in the rectangular array of boxes? __2__

8. How many boxes in all are in the rectangular array of boxes? __6__

Copyright © Houghton Mifflin Company. All rights reserved.

Use with text pages 88–89.

Patterns in Multiplication and Division

Practice using the multiplication table by answering these questions.

columns

X	0	1	2	3	4	5	6	7	8
0	0	0	0	0	0	0	0	0	0
1	0	1	2	3	4	5	6	7	8
2	0	2	4	6	8	10	12	14	16
3	0	3	6	9	12	15	18	21	24
4	0	4	8	12	16	20	24	28	32
5	0	5	10	15	20	25	30	35	40
6	0	6	12	18	24	30	36	42	48
7	0	7	14	21	28	35	42	49	56
8	0	8	16	24	32	40	48	56	64

rows

1. Look in the column under 2 for the product of 2 and 4. What is the product? __8__ Circle it.

2. Complete this multiplication sentence: 2 × 4 = __8__.

3. Look in the column under 4 for the product of 4 and 2. What is the product? __8__ Circle it.

4. Complete this multiplication sentence: 4 × __2__ = 8.

5. Look at the two multiplication sentences you completed. How are they different? _The order of the factors is different._

_____

How are they the same? _The factors themselves and the product are the same._

6. Which property says that the order of factors in a multiplication problem can be changed without making the answer different? _commutative property_

7. How did the order of factors change in the two multiplication sentences?

The position of the two factors was switched.

Was the answer different when the change was made? _No._

8. Do these multiplication sentences show how the Commutative Property works? _Yes. They show that the product is the same_

How do they do this? _even when the order of factors is different._

Copyright © Houghton Mifflin Company. All rights reserved.

Use with text pages 90–91.

Multiplication and Division
Facts to Five

Read the expressions and their explanations.

to five	whole numbers from 0 to 5
skip count	count by 2, by 3, or by some other number greater than 1
double 2	twice as much as 2
repeated subtraction	subtract the same number over and over until you reach 0
related multiplication fact	multiplication sentence with the same factors as a division sentence

Label each example with an expression from the box.

multiplication facts to five	**skip count**	**use doubles**
use repeated subtraction	**use a related multiplication fact**	

1. $3 \times 4 = 12$
$6 \times 4 = ?$
6 is the double of 3.
$6 \times 4 = 12 \times 2$

use doubles
_____

2. $12 - 3 = 9$
$9 - 3 = 6$
$6 - 3 = 3$
$3 - 3 = 0$

use repeated
subtraction
_____

3. 4, 8, 12, 16, 20

skip count
_____

4. $18 \div 3 =$ Think:
$3 \times \quad = 18$
$3 \times 6 = 18$

use a related
multiplication fact
_____

5. $0 \times 5 = 0$ $1 \times 5 = 5$ $2 \times 5 = 10$
$3 \times 5 = 15$ $4 \times 5 = 20$ $5 \times 5 = 25$

multiplication
facts to five
_____

Copyright © Houghton Mifflin Company. All rights reserved.

Use with text pages 92–93.

Multiplication and Division Facts to Ten

Read the paragraphs. Pay attention to the words in bold type.

Rex, Anna, and Kim will **put on** a puppet show tomorrow. They will present the performance at 4 o'clock. Rex bought a kit for a puppet theater last week. He put it together yesterday. The theater was not difficult to **assemble.** Anna bought fancy tickets to sell. The tickets **come in packages of** 20. Anna counted the tickets to make sure there really were 20 tickets in each package.

Kim used a computer program to make a poster. He typed in the name of the show. He also put in the date, time, and location of the performance, and the cost of a ticket. The computer program took this **input** and created a design. The **output** was a colorful poster. The poster came out of the printer slowly, but it looked wonderful!

Draw lines to match each term to its meaning.

1. **input**   put together

2. **output**   give a performance

3. **assemble**   what is put into something

4. **come in packages of**   what comes out of something

5. **put on a show**   are wrapped in sets of

Copyright © Houghton Mifflin Company. All rights reserved.

Use with text pages 94–96.

Name _____   Date _____

Multiply and Divide With 11 and 12

Read the expressions and their explanations.

column for 10	the products that appear below 10 in the table
11 facts	all the multiplication facts for 11
row for 12	the products that appear beside 12 in the table
multiples of 6	all the products of multiplication facts for 6

Label each circled item on the multiplication table. Use the phrases in bold type above.

multiples of 5

column for 10 **1.**

multiples of 6 **2.**

11 facts **3.**

row for 12 **4.**

X	0	1	2	3	4	5	6	7	8	9	10	11	12
0	0	0	0	0	0	0	0	0	0	0	0	0	0
1	0	1	2	3	4	5	6	7	8	9	10	11	12
2	0	2	4	6	8	10	12	14	16	18	20	22	24
3	0	3	6	9	12	15	18	21	24	27	30	33	36
4	0	4	8	12	16	20	24	28	32	36	40	44	48
5	0	5	10	15	20	25	30	35	40	45	50	55	60
6	0	6	12	18	24	30	36	42	48	54	60	66	72
7	0	7	14	21	28	35	42	49	56	63	70	77	84
8	0	8	16	24	32	40	48	56	64	72	80	88	96
9	0	9	18	27	36	45	54	63	72	81	90	99	108
10	0	10	20	30	40	50	60	70	80	90	100	110	120
11	0	11	22	33	44	55	66	77	88	99	110	121	132
12	0	12	24	36	48	60	72	84	96	108	120	132	144

Circle these on the multiplication table. Label each one.

column for 9

row for 10

5. row for 10

6. column for 9

7. multiples of 5

Copyright © Houghton Mifflin Company. All rights reserved.

Use with text pages 98–99.

Multiply Three Factors

Look at the pictures. Read the captions.

upright bass

jazz trio

color guard

marching band

Solve the riddles.

1. We play music outdoors. We don't stand still. _marching band_

2. We carry our nation's flag. We make sure it is displayed in the correct way.
   color guard

3. I am a very large instrument. I look like a guitar. I have four strings.
   upright bass

4. Three of us play together. We play music with a lot of rhythm. _jazz trio_

Copyright © Houghton Mifflin Company. All rights reserved.

Use with text pages 100–101.

Name _____ Date _____

Division With Remainders

Read each word. Look at the picture that shows its meaning.

dragon

acrobat

fan

tea set

balancing

performance

Write a word from above to complete each sentence.

1. An ___acrobat___ is a performer who flies through the air and balances in difficult positions.

2. A ___tea set___ is used for serving hot tea to guests.

3. A ___dragon___ is an imaginary animal with big teeth and a long tail.

4. A ___fan___ can be waved to make a little breeze on a hot day.

5. A ___performance___ is a show or activity done in front of an audience.

6. If you are using your muscles to keep something from falling,

   you are ___balancing___ it.

Copyright © Houghton Mifflin Company. All rights reserved.

Use with text pages 102–103.

Name _____ Date _____

Problem-Solving Decision: Choose the Operation

Read each problem. Look at the words in bold type.
Look also at the word that tells what operation you must
do to solve the problem.

Sam has 4 juggling balls and 3 juggling oranges. **How many** things for juggling does Sam have?

addition 4 + 3

Anita has 3 bags. There are 2 bowling pins **in each** bag. **How many** bowling pins does she have **in all** 3 bags?

multiplication 3 × 2

Hassan has 5 juggling balls. Lorena has 6 juggling balls. **How many more** juggling balls does Lorena have?

subtraction 6 − 5

Cody has 8 rings. He wants to juggle **the same number in each** hand. How many rings will he juggle **in each** hand?

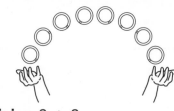

division 8 ÷ 2

Read each problem below. Look at the words in bold type.
Write whether you would use *addition,* *subtraction,*
***multiplication,* or** *division* **to solve each.**

1. Irma has 6 bowling pins and 2 sacks. She wants to put **the same number** of pins **in each** sack. How many pins will she put **in each** sack?

division
_____

2. Trinh has 4 bowls. She has 2 oranges **in each** bowl. **How many** oranges does she have **in all**?

multiplication
_____

3. Stavros has 4 bowling pins. Elias has 7 bowling pins. **How many more** pins does Elias have?

subtraction
_____

4. Diana has 3 juggling rings and 5 juggling plates. **How many** things for juggling does she have?

addition
_____

Copyright © Houghton Mifflin Company. All rights reserved.

Use with text page 104.

Name _____   Date _____

Order of Operations

**Read the paragraph. Think about the meanings of
the words in bold type.**

The people in this **patrol** are looking for **green turtles.** Green
turtles are a type of sea turtle. A mother green turtle digs a hole
on a sandy **beach.** This hole is a **nest,** a place for her to lay
eggs. After she lays her eggs, the mother sea turtle covers them
with sand to **protect** them. The sand keeps them safely hidden.
The baby turtles that hatch from the eggs are called **hatchlings.**

**Draw lines to match the words to the phrases that
tell about them.**

1. patrol   an area at the edge of the sea

2. beach   to keep safe from harm

3. green turtle   a group that looks or watches

4. nest   a baby turtle

5. protect   a large turtle that lives in the ocean

6. hatchling   a place for laying eggs

Copyright © Houghton Mifflin Company. All rights reserved.   **Use with text pages 110–111.**

Words Into Expressions

Read the definitions.

endanger	to put at risk
endangered	at risk of becoming extinct
danger	something likely to cause harm
dangerous	likely to cause harm
wild	not tame
wilderness	an area where almost no people live
vary	to make changes
variable	a symbol that can stand for different numbers

Underline the correct word in each sentence.

1. Many people want to protect (endangered, danger) animals so these creatures do not disappear from earth.

2. Visitors to parks should not go near animals that are (wild, wilderness).

3. In Yellowstone National Park the weather can (vary, variable), so visitors should bring jackets.

4. Going into the den of an animal is very (danger, dangerous).

5. If you know how much each visitor must pay but you don't know how many visitors will come, you might use a (vary, variable) for the number of visitors and write an expression.

6. A big fire can (danger, endanger) many animals.

7. Rangers are trained in (wilderness, wild) safety.

8. Red signs usually warn people about (endanger, danger).

Copyright © Houghton Mifflin Company. All rights reserved.

Use with text pages 112–114.

Compare Expressions

Read the definitions.

equal	the same value as
unequal	not the same value as
equation	equal expressions connected by an equals sign
equals sign (=)	a symbol indicating that two things have the same value
equality	mathematical statement that one thing equals another
inequality	mathematical statement that one thing does not equal another

Follow the instructions.

1. Circle the **equals sign.**

$6 + (4 - 2) \; ⊜ \; 8$ $6 + (4 - 3) \neq 8$

2. Circle the **equality.**

$\boxed{5 - (3 + 1) = 0 + 1}$ $5 - (2 + 1) > 0 + 1$

3. Circle the **equation.**

$\boxed{6 + y = 21}$ $3n + 8$

4. Circle the **inequality.**

$6 + 5 = 5 + 6$ $\boxed{5 + 4 + 1 < 5 + 6}$

5. Circle the amounts that are **equal.**

$\boxed{1 + 2 + 3 \text{ and } 3 + 2 + 1}$ $1 + 2 + 3 \text{ and } 4 + 5 + 6$

6. Circle the amounts that are **unequal.**

$15 - 7 \text{ and } 13 - 5$ $\boxed{14 - 8 \text{ and } 15 - 7}$

Copyright © Houghton Mifflin Company. All rights reserved.

Use with text pages 116–117.

Variables and Equations

Look at the pictures and the labels.

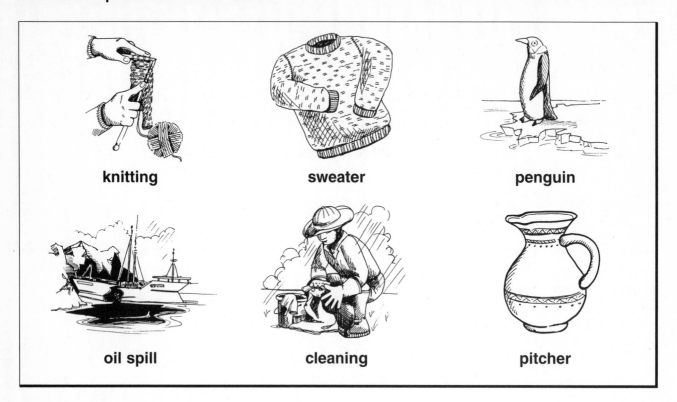

knitting   sweater   penguin

oil spill   cleaning   pitcher

Write a word from above to complete each sentence.

1. On a cold day you might wear a ___sweater___ to keep warm.

2. ___Knitting___ is a way to make yarn into clothing.

3. A ___penguin___ is a black-and-white bird that lives in cold places.

4. Soap is used for ___cleaning___ many things.

5. When a ship carrying oil smashes into rocks, the result can be a big, messy ___oil spill___.

6. You can fill a ___pitcher___ with milk and put it on the table for everyone to share.

Copyright © Houghton Mifflin Company. All rights reserved.

Use with text pages 118–120.

Problem-Solving Strategy:
Write an Equation

Read this paragraph. Pay attention to how the words in bold type are used.

Lisa wants to **adopt** a dog. She will become its owner and take good care of it. She will make sure the dog gets **exercise** by letting it run in the park. On cold days Lisa will wear a **scarf** around her neck. Lisa will be glad to pay a **fee** for a **rabies shot** for the dog. Although the needle will hurt the dog a little, the shot will keep it healthy. Lisa will train the dog not to run or jump inside. If the dog knocks over a **flowerpot** with a pretty plant growing in it, Lisa's mother will not be happy.

Draw a line to connect the words with their definitions.

1. fee   "activity to stay healthy"

2. exercise   "medicine given with a needle to prevent a disease"

3. flowerpot   "cloth to keep the neck warm"

4. adopt   "an amount of money that is paid for a service"

5. rabies shot   "container for growing a plant"

6. scarf   "to agree to care for"

Copyright © Houghton Mifflin Company. All rights reserved.

Use with text pages 122–125.

Name _____ Date _____

Function Tables

Read the cartoons and the information below.

In English, many verbs have noun forms that end with *-ation* or *-tion*. For example, the verb *conserve,* meaning "to save," has the related noun form *conservation,* meaning "the process of saving."

Write a noun from the box to complete each sentence.

solution	operation	adoption	collection	expression

1. A group of things you have collected is a ___collection___ .

2. A way of solving a problem is a ___solution___ .

3. Something that expresses an idea or a feeling is an ___expression___ .

4. If you decide to adopt a dog or cat, you go through the process of ___adoption___ .

5. When a doctor operates to fix something in a person's body, the process is called an ___operation___ .

Copyright © Houghton Mifflin Company. All rights reserved.

Use with text pages 126–127.

Name _____ Date _____

Problem-Solving Decision: Explain Your Solution

Look at this chart. It shows words used to tell how often something happens.

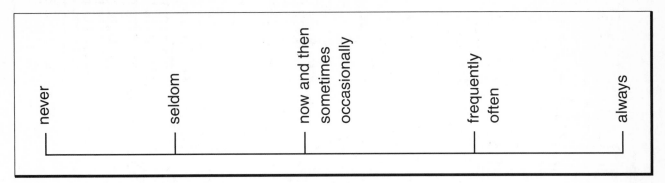

Write words from the chart to answer the questions.

1. How often do you walk on the ceiling?

   _____ never _____

2. How often do you drink milk at dinner?

   _____

3. On cold days, how often do you wear warm clothes?

   _____

4. How often do you play tag at recess?

   _____

5. On weekends, how often do you ride your bike?

   _____

6. How often do your aunts, uncles, and cousins come to visit on holidays?

   _____

2–6: Answers will vary but should reflect understanding of the meanings of the relative terms being taught.

Copyright © Houghton Mifflin Company. All rights reserved.

Use with text page 128.

Name _____   Date _____

Multiply Multiples of 10, 100, and 1,000

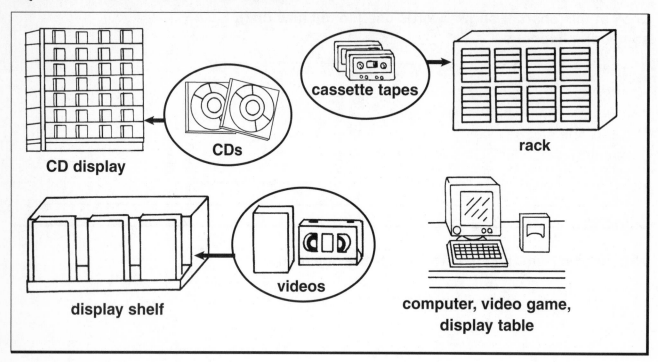

CD display

CDs

cassette tapes

rack

display shelf

videos

computer, video game,
display table

Fill each blank with a term from the box.

CDs	cassette tapes	computer	videos	video game
CD display	display table	rack	display shelf	

1. The videos are on the ___display shelf___.

2. The computer is on the ___display table___.

3. The cassette tapes are on the ___rack___.

4. The video game is on the ___display table___.

5. The CDs are in the ___CD display___.

6. The display shelf holds ___videos___.

7. The display table holds a ___computer___ and a ___video game___.

8. The rack holds ___cassette tapes___.

9. The CD display holds ___CDs___.

Copyright © Houghton Mifflin Company. All rights reserved.

Use with text pages 146–147.

Estimate Products

Read the definitions.

kindness	being helpful
donate	give as a gift to be helpful
charity	an organization that helps people in need
random	having no pattern
craft kit	set of materials for making something by hand
grand opening	celebration of the first day a store is open
shelter	a building where people without homes can sleep

Complete these sentences. Use words from the list above.

1. Luba wanted to make flowers out of paper, so she bought a ___craft kit___.

2. When the river rose and flooded their home, the Cliftons stayed
   in a ___shelter___.

3. Norberto helps out at a home for older people, and the people there are grateful
   for his ___kindness___.

4. The American Red Cross is a ___charity___ that helps people affected by floods,
   fires, and other disasters.

5. Instead of planning a shopping trip, Victor and his sister made
   ___random___ stops at stores.

6. The Park family decorated their new store with balloons for its ___grand opening___.

7. Mac and Ruthann will ___donate___ clothing and blankets to help families
   in need.

Copyright © Houghton Mifflin Company. All rights reserved.

Use with text pages 148–149.

Name _____   Date _____

Model Multiplication by One-Digit Numbers

The plural is the form of a word you use to talk about two or more things. Look at how each word below forms its plural.

shelf → shelves	city → cities	zero → zeros
yo-yo → yo-yos	video → videos	potato → potatoes
class → classes	school → schools	symbol → symbols
box → boxes	half → halves	charity → charities
grandchild → grandchildren	woman → women	tomato → tomatoes

Look again at the plural forms above. Write each plural in the box that tells how it was formed.

Order of some answers may vary.

---

s was added to a word that does not end in *o*.

1. schools
2. symbols

---

es was added to a word that does not end in *o*.

3. classes
4. boxes

---

y was changed to *i*, and *es* was added.

5. cities
6. charities

---

f was changed to *v*, and *es* was added.

7. shelves
8. halves

The plural was not formed by adding *s* or *es*.

9. grandchildren
10. women

---

s was added to a word that ends in *o*.

11. yo-yos
12. videos
13. zeros

---

es was added to a word that ends in *o*.

14. potatoes
15. tomatoes

Copyright © Houghton Mifflin Company. All rights reserved.

Use with text pages 150–151.

Multiply Two-Digit Numbers by One-Digit Numbers

To **restate** a problem means "to say it in a different way." Sometimes restating a problem in a series of sentences can make it easier to understand and solve.

Read these problems. See how they have been restated.

Problem: How does thinking of 39 as 30 + 9 help Greg multiply?

restated:

- Greg needs to multiply a number by 39.

- He thinks of 39 as 30 + 9.

- Why does this help Greg solve the problem?

Problem: What do you think happens to a product when you double one of its factors?

restated:

- Think of a multiplication sentence with two factors.

- Double one of the factors.

- What happens to the product?

Restate each problem below to make it easier to understand and solve.

1. How does thinking of 19 as 20 − 1 help Camellia multiply?
   restated:

   Camellia needs to multiply 19 by another number. She thinks of 19 as 20 − 1. Why does this help Camellia solve the problem?

2. What do you think happens to a product when you triple one of its factors?
   restated:

   Think of a multiplication sentence with two factors. Triple one of the factors. What happens to the product?

Copyright © Houghton Mifflin Company. All rights reserved.

Use with text pages 152–154.

Problem-Solving Strategy:
Guess and Check

Read the terms and the definitions.

twice as many	double the amount
the same amount	an amount that is equal
how many more (than)	what amount greater (than)
how much longer (than)	what length more (than)
altogether	in total
guess	think about what the answer is likely to be

Find the bold term above that tells about each item.
Write that bold term on the line.

1. You measure two things.
   You compare their lengths.

   how much longer (than)

2. You find the sum of several numbers.

   altogether

3. You multiply a number by 2.

   twice as many

4. You try out a number you think could be the
   answer before working to solve a problem.

   guess

5. You compare the values on
   both sides of an equation.

   the same amount

6. You count the items in two groups.
   You compare the numbers.

   how many more (than)

Copyright © Houghton Mifflin Company. All rights reserved.

Use with text pages 156–158.

Multiply Three-Digit Numbers by One-Digit Numbers

Many words in English have more than one meaning.
Read the dictionary entry below.

order *noun* 1. a certain sequence 2. a neat arrangement 3. a request for a certain item or group of items 4. a statement telling someone that they have to do something
verb 5. to put in a sequence 6. to make neat 7. to ask for a certain item from a company or in a restaurant 8. to tell someone they must do something

Look at how *order* is used in each of these sentences. Write the definition that matches its use. (*Hint: Order* is used as a noun in all these sentences.)

1. Your **order** will be brought to your table when everything has been cooked.
   a request for a certain item or group of items

2. The leader gave an **order,** and everyone did what he said. a statement telling someone that they have to do something

3. Jai has put her sister's room in **order.** a neat arrangement

4. Put the shoes in **order,** from largest to smallest. a certain sequence

Look at how *order* is used in each of these sentences. Write the definition that matches its use. (*Hint: Order* is used as a verb in all these sentences.)

5. Maud **ordered** a fried egg. to ask for a certain item from a company or in a restaurant

6. Bill **ordered** the streamers from the shortest to the longest. to put in a sequence

7. Tara **ordered** her brother to put down her doll. to tell someone they must do something

8. Reggie must **order** his room before his grandparents visit. to make neat

Copyright © Houghton Mifflin Company. All rights reserved.

Use with text pages 160–163.

Multiply Greater Numbers

Read these definitions.

train route	the path that railroad tracks follow
one-way trip	trip from one place to another, but not back
round trip	trip from one place to another and then back

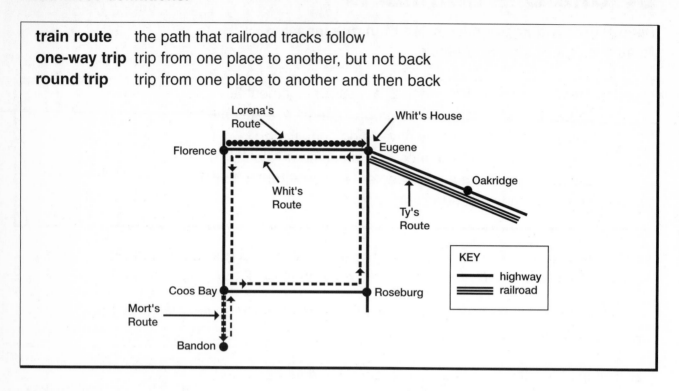

This map shows the routes, or paths, that four students traveled. Read each description. Write the name of the student whose trip is being described.

1. This student rode along the train route from Eugene through Oakridge.

   ___Ty___

2. This student took a one-way trip along a highway. ___Lorena___

3. This student took a trip to three cities and ended up back home. ___Whit___

4. This student took a round trip between two cities. ___Mort___

Use the map to help you complete these sentences.

5. Whit traveled from ___Eugene___ to Florence, from Florence to ___Coos Bay___, from ___Coos Bay___ to Roseburg, and from Roseburg to ___Eugene___.

6. Mort lives in Coos Bay. He traveled to ___Bandon___ and back.

Copyright © Houghton Mifflin Company. All rights reserved.

Use with text pages 164–166.

Patterns With Multiples of 10, 100, and 1,000

Read these explanations.

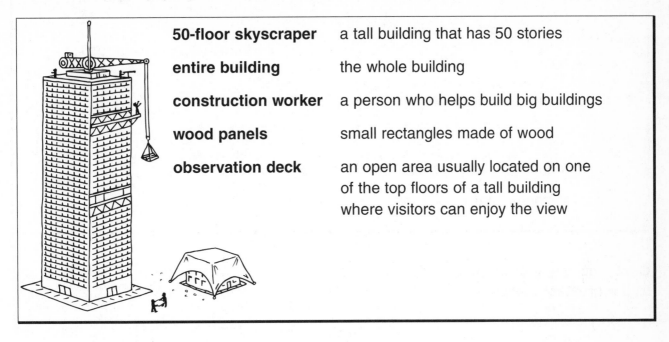

50-floor skyscraper	a tall building that has 50 stories
entire building	the whole building
construction worker	a person who helps build big buildings
wood panels	small rectangles made of wood
observation deck	an open area usually located on one of the top floors of a tall building where visitors can enjoy the view

Use words in the box to make the sentences tell about the buildings.

50-floor skyscraper wood panels	entire building observation deck	construction worker

1. At the top of the tall building is an ___observation deck___. People can see the whole city from there.

2. The workers have put a tent over the small building. The tent covers the ___entire building___.

3. Two workers are carrying ___wood panels___ into the tall building.

4. The tall building is a ___50-floor skyscraper___.

5. A ___construction worker___ is walking on a beam high in the building.

Copyright © Houghton Mifflin Company. All rights reserved.

Use with text pages 172–173.

Estimate Products

Read this information. Look at the examples.

Rounding to the greatest place means rounding to the place farthest to the left.

It means rounding **to the nearest 10** for a 2-digit number.

47 → 50   83 → 80

It means rounding **to the nearest 100** for a 3-digit number.

265 → 300   511 → 500

It means rounding **to the nearest 1000** for a 4-digit number.

6926 → 7000   4381 → 4000

Circle the way you would round each number to the greatest place.

1. 229

   to the nearest 10   (to the nearest 100)   to the nearest 1000

2. 46

   (to the nearest 10)   to the nearest 100   to the nearest 1000

3. 5951

   to the nearest 10   to the nearest 100   (to the nearest 1000)

4. 946

   to the nearest 10   (to the nearest 100)   to the nearest 1000

5. 4808

   to the nearest 10   to the nearest 100   (to the nearest 1000)

Copyright © Houghton Mifflin Company. All rights reserved.

Use with text pages 174–175.

Model Multiplication

In English, you can add the suffix *-tion* to many verbs to make nouns that name processes. Read these definitions.

Distribute means "to give out in portions."

Distribution means "the process of giving out in portions."

Separate means "to set apart, or move things away from each other."

Separation means "the process of setting apart, or moving things away from each other."

Write *distribute*, *distribution*, *separate*, or *separation* to complete each sentence.

1. In a zoo, strong fences _____ separate _____ the animals from the visitors.

2. This _____ separation _____ is necessary to keep the animals and the visitors from harming each other.

3. Zoo workers _____ distribute _____ food to all the animals.

4. The _____ distribution _____ must be done carefully, because each animal needs a particular kind of food.

Circle the correct definition.

Distributive means   "having to do with setting apart"

"having to do with making portions"

Copyright © Houghton Mifflin Company. All rights reserved.

Use with text pages 176–177.

Multiply 2 Two-Digit Numbers

Look at the pictures. Read the explanations.

A **mineral** is a natural material that comes from the earth. Metals, coal, and oil are minerals.

Amber is ancient tree sap that became solid over time. It is yellow in color and is used in jewelry.

A **fossil** is an ancient bone, footprint, or leaf imprint that has become rock, or part of a rock.

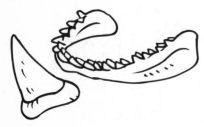

This **shark's tooth** came from the jaw of a great white shark, a fierce hunter of other fish.

An **ammonite** is the fossil shell of a sea animal that lived millions of years ago.

A **geode** is a hollow rock with crystals on its inside wall.

Draw lines to match words with the descriptions that fit them.

1. amber   found in the mouth of a meat-eating fish

2. shark's tooth   a rock that is pretty when cut in half

3. ammonite   gold, silver, iron, copper, petroleum

4. fossil   a pretty yellow stone in a necklace

5. geode   the home of an ancient ocean creature

6. minerals   something from an ancient plant or animal preserved in stone

Copyright © Houghton Mifflin Company. All rights reserved.

Use with text pages 178–180.

Problem-Solving Decision:
Reasonable Answers

Read the information.

$5.00	$5,000.00
It is **reasonable** to pay $5.00 for a package of Valentine's Day cards to send to friends. Paying $5.00 for a package of cards **makes sense**.	It is **unreasonable** to pay $5,000.00 for a package of Valentine's Day cards. Paying $5,000.00 for a package of cards **doesn't make sense**.

Write _reasonable_ or _unreasonable_ in each blank.

1. Roger is not going to school because he has the flu. It is _reasonable_ _____ for Roger to stay home.

2. Joel is not going to school because he wants to play with his new puppy. It is _unreasonable_ _____ for Joel to stay at home.

3. Alizia plans to paint 100 pictures every day. It is _unreasonable_ _____ for Alizia to plan to paint 100 pictures every day.

4. Verna plans to paint 1 picture every day. It is _reasonable_ _____ for Verna to plan to paint 1 picture every day.

5. Marcus plans to start a dog-walking business. He will charge $700.00 to walk a dog for 1 hour. It is _unreasonable_ _____ for Marcus to charge that much.

6. Luis is starting a dog-walking business. He charges $7.00 to walk a dog for 1 hour. It is _reasonable_ _____ for Luis to charge that much.

Copyright © Houghton Mifflin Company. All rights reserved.

Use with text page 182.

Multiply Three-Digit Numbers by Two-Digit Numbers

Read this dialogue.

Interviewer:	Today we will talk about exercise—moving our muscles to keep our bodies strong. Officer Williams, how do you **get exercise**?
Officer Williams:	I get my exercise **on the job.** I walk at least two miles every day while I am working.
Interviewer:	Walking is good exercise. How many days do you work **in a year**?
Officer Williams:	I work about 250 days every year.
Interviewer:	Well, if you work 250 days in a year, and you walk at least 2 miles a day, that means you walk at least 500 miles each year. That's a lot! Now, Mrs. Alvarez, how do you get exercise?
Mrs. Alvarez:	I get exercise while I work, too. I work in a stock room—a place with boxes of things people buy. When I **fill an order,** I have to lift boxes very carefully and then carry them to the counter.
Interviewer:	You mean you get the items a customer has asked for?

Match the phrases to their meanings.

1. get exercise   while working

2. in a year   get the items a customer wants

3. on the job   during a 12-month period

4. fill an order   move muscles to stay healthy

Copyright © Houghton Mifflin Company. All rights reserved.

Use with text pages 184–185.

Multiply Greater Numbers

Look at the picture. Read the caption.

This is George Hernandez. He designs Web sites. He is now designing a Web site for an online auction store.

Circle the pictures that answer the questions.

1. What kind of Web site is Mr. Hernandez designing?

2. Which picture shows how Mr. Hernandez goes online?

3. Which picture shows the kind of hit Mr. Hernandez wants on the Web site he is creating?

4. Which picture shows the part of an online auction store you might visit with a parent?

Copyright © Houghton Mifflin Company. All rights reserved.

Use with text pages 186–188.

Model Division

Read this explanation.

In math, **divide** means "to separate into equal parts" or "to put in equal groups."

The process of dividing is called **division.** In a division problem, the process of dividing is shown in numbers. The total number being divided is called the **dividend.** The number of groups or portions the number is being divided into is called the **divisor.** The answer— the size of each portion or the number in each group—is called the **quotient.** Any amount left over when the equal portions are made is called the **remainder.**

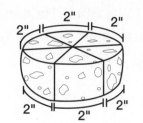

$12 \div 6 = 2$

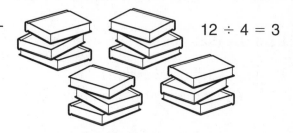

$12 \div 4 = 3$

Write words from the box to fill the blanks.

| divide | division | dividend | divisor | quotient | remainder |

6)‾12‾   This is a ___division___ problem. In this problem you must

___divide___ 12 by 6. The number that must be divided, 12, is

called the ___dividend___. The number it must be divided by, 6,

is called the ___divisor___.

3
4)‾12‾   This division problem has been solved. The answer, 3, is called the

___quotient___.

3 r1
4)‾12‾   This division problem has 1 left over. This amount is called the

___remainder___.

Copyright © Houghton Mifflin Company. All rights reserved.

Use with text pages 206–207.

Divide With Remainders

Read this information.

Model is a word with many meanings. It can be used as a noun, a verb, or an adjective. The dictionary entry below gives the noun meanings.

mod•el (mod′l) noun. 1. a small copy of something: This *model* of a race car is 6 inches long. 2. a tiny example of something not yet made: The builder showed the family a *model* of the house he planned to build. 3. a style or design: This year's *model* of the Speedycar is much better look-ing than last year's model. 4. a person serving as a subject for an artist: Rhonda asked her friend Beth to be a *model* for a painting she wanted to make. 5. a person paid to display clothes by wearing them: Helen will be a *model* in the fashion show tomorrow.

Match each picture to the definition that fits it.

1. a small copy of something

2.  a tiny example of something not yet made

3. a style or design

4. a person serving as a subject for an artist

5.  a person paid to display clothes by wearing them

Copyright © Houghton Mifflin Company. All rights reserved.

Use with text pages 208–209.

Problem-Solving Application:
Interpret Remainders

Read these definitions.

post card	a card used for sending a short message through the mail
exhibit	a display
on display	being shown to people
tour	to make a trip through a place for the purpose of seeing it
demonstration	a show of how something works
scrapbook	a book with blank pages for pasting pictures in
printing plant	a building with machines that print words and pictures on paper
museum	a building in which art or historic items are displayed

Complete these paragraphs. Fill in the blanks with words from the boxes.

tour	**printing plant**	**demonstration**

Mrs. Napoleon's class is studying newspapers. Today

they are going to visit a _____ to see how

newspapers are printed. There they will see a _____

of a printing press. After that, the students will _____

the newspaper office to see where the writers and editors work.

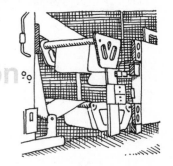

on display	**museum**	**exhibit**	**scrapbook**	**post card**

Mr. Ortega's class is studying art. They are going to visit

a _____ to see the famous paintings that are

_____ there. They will also see an _____

of children's art. After that, each child will be given a

_____ with a picture of the museum on it. Each child

can send the card to a friend, or put it in a _____.

Copyright © Houghton Mifflin Company. All rights reserved.

Use with text pages 210–212.

Regroup in Division

Read the explanation and the definitions that follow.

The prefix *re-* usually means "back" or "again." Knowing this can help you figure out the meanings of many words.

regroup	to group again; to put into new groups
rearrange	to arrange again; to arrange in a new way
repay	to pay back; to pay people money you owe them
recount	to count again
replace	to put or give something in place of something that has been lost or broken
refund	to give back money
reorder	to order again

When you are dividing, you can regroup ten as 10 ones to help you solve the problem.

Complete the sentences below. Fill in the blanks with words in bold type.

1. To make sure that the votes have been counted correctly, two students will ___recount___ the votes.

2. Edda Mae ordered pencils and pens for the office. They are almost gone, so she must ___reorder___ some soon.

3. The big show has been canceled. The ticket company will ___refund___ money to everyone who bought a ticket.

4. Derek grouped the blocks in sets of 10 to solve the division problem. He must ___regroup___ some of the blocks in order to get the answer.

5. Sveta broke a flowerpot. She must ___replace___ it.

6. Keenan borrowed five dollars from his brother last week. Keenan has now earned ten dollars, so he can ___repay___ his brother.

7. Greta does not like where the chairs and the tables have been placed. She will ___rearrange___ the furniture so it looks better.

Copyright © Houghton Mifflin Company. All rights reserved.

Use with text pages 214–216.

Divide Multiples of 10, 100, and 1,000

Read these explanations.

Today it is December 1, 2003.

Six months ago it was June 1, 2003.

After one year it will be December 1 again.

If you are fifty years old, it means you have had a birthday in **each of 50 years.**

If you go to the store **every week,** it means you go to the store at least once every seven days.

If you work for **a full week,** you work all seven days in that week.

Match each phrase with its meaning.

1. a full week   seven days in the future

2. 10 years ago   seven days in a row

3. every week   at least one time in a period of seven days

4. each of 10 years   a date 10 years in the past

5. after one week   every year in a period of 10 years

Copyright © Houghton Mifflin Company. All rights reserved.

Use with text pages 218–219.

Name _____ Date _____

Estimate Quotients

Read these explanations.

> **Estimate** means "to use what you know to make a good guess at an answer."
>
> **Find the exact amount** means "to figure out the precise number."

Some terms in the box tell about estimating. Others tell about finding the exact amount. Write each term on any line in the web where it belongs.

how much	about how much	guess	calculate
how many	about how many	almost	precisely
estimated quotient	exact quotient	possible	certain

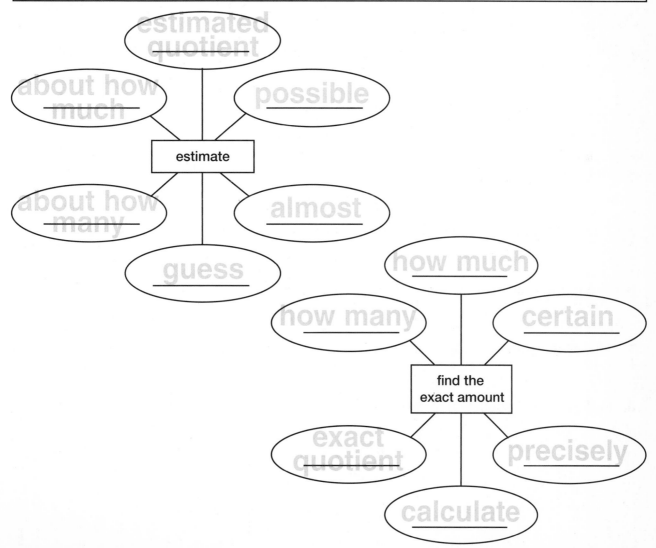

Copyright © Houghton Mifflin Company. All rights reserved.

Use with text pages 220–222.

Three-Digit Quotients

**In English, some words sound the same but are spelled
differently and have different meanings. Read the
dictionary entries below.**

---

fair *adjective* 1. pleasant to look at: a *fair maiden.* 2. free of clouds
or storms: *a fair sky.* 3. showing honesty: a *fair judgment.* 4. neither
good nor bad: *The movie was only fair.*

fair *noun* 1. a gathering for buying and selling things. 2. a large
exhibition, often with games and rides.

fare *noun* 1. the money a passenger pays. 2. food and drink.

Write *fair* or *fare* to complete each sentence.

1. The rules were not _____, so Rick stopped playing the game.

2. The _____ at the hotel was very tasty.

3. Nina paid the _____ to the driver and then found a seat on the bus.

4. Nori won a prize for his strawberries at the county _____.

5. Alma painted a picture of a brave warrior and a _____ maiden.

6. The judge made a _____ decision.

7. The ballplayers had hoped for _____ skies, but instead a storm came in.

8. Sari is a good soccer player but only a _____ basketball player.

Copyright © Houghton Mifflin Company. All rights reserved.

Use with text pages 228–229.

Place the First Digit of the Quotient

The word *left* is the form of *leave* used to talk about the past. *Left* is used in several expressions with special meanings. Read these definitions.

left over	not used; remaining	**left behind**	not taken on a trip
left out	not included	**left alone**	not bothered

Write an expression from the box to complete each sentence.

left over	left out	left behind	left alone

1. Reyna told her noisy little brother that she wanted to be
   <u>left alone</u> .

2. After giving everyone an orange, Wilson had 3 oranges <u>left over</u> .

3. Cammie cared for 2 cats <u>left behind</u> by a family that moved to Ohio.

4. A child <u>left out</u> of a game usually feels sad.

5. Jan discovered that she had <u>left behind</u> the sunglasses she needed for her vacation.

6. The sentence did not make sense because a word had been <u>left out</u> .

> **This store will at 5 P.M.**

7. Khalid likes to be <u>left alone</u> when he does his math homework.

8. When Penny put her photos into 5 groups of the same size, she had 3 photos <u>left over</u> .

Copyright © Houghton Mifflin Company. All rights reserved.

Use with text pages 230–233.

Divide Money

Read this information.

Jorge and Scott must divide $1.80 evenly.

First they **estimate** the answer. $1.80 is close to $2.00. $2.00 divided by 2 equals $1.00. Each boy will get about one dollar.

Next, they **divide** as if they were dividing whole numbers.

```
     90
2)$1.80
```

Then they write the **dollar sign** to the left of the answer, and put a **decimal point** above the decimal point in the dividend.

```
    $.90
2)$1.80
```

The answer is 90 cents. That is close to the estimate of 1 dollar, so it is a **reasonable** answer.

Use words from the box to fill the blanks.

divide	dollar sign	decimal point	reasonable	estimate

Iris and Sari must divide $3.90 evenly.

1. First, they ___estimate___ the amount each of them will get.

2. Next, they write the numbers as a division problem.
   They ___divide___ $3.90 by 2.

3. After that, they write a ___dollar sign___ to the left of the quotient.

4. Then they place a ___decimal point___ above the decimal point in the dividend.

5. Finally, they check the quotient against their estimate to make sure the answer is ___reasonable___.

Copyright © Houghton Mifflin Company. All rights reserved.

Use with text pages 234–237.

Zeros in the Quotient

Read these definitions.

whale watch	a trip to try to see whales
tour	a trip to see certain places or things
tour manager	a person who organizes tours
binoculars	special glasses that let you see things that are far away
tourist	a person who travels to a place to see interesting things

Complete the crossword puzzle. Use the words in bold type above.

Across

3. an instrument used to view faraway things

5. a woman or man who sets up trips to interesting places

Down

1. a voyage in search of huge ocean animals

2. someone who goes somewhere to look at the sights

4. a journey to interesting places

Copyright © Houghton Mifflin Company. All rights reserved.

Use with text pages 238–239.

Problem-Solving Strategy:
Work Backward

Look at the pictures. Read the descriptions.

An **aquarium** is a place where you can see all kinds of fish.

Tropical fish are fish that live in warm parts of the ocean.

Jellyfish are sea animals with bodies you can see through.

A **leafy sea dragon** is a small sea animal that is related to sea horses.

A **starfish** is a star-shaped animal that lives at the edge of the ocean.

An **angelfish** is a colorful tropical fish.

Solve the riddles. Use the words in bold type above.

1. My name might make you think I am all white, but I am brightly colored. I am an ___angelfish___ .

2. I never eat anything, but I am full of fish. I am an ___aquarium___ .

3. We are fish that like nice warm water, but we do not like to take baths. We are ___tropical fish___ .

4. The beginning of my name makes me sound like a tree. The end of my name makes me sound like a monster. I look like a plant, but I am a sea animal. I am a ___leafy sea dragon___ .

5. My name makes me sound like you could spread me on toast. I don't come in a jar, though. I live in the ocean. I am a ___jellyfish___ .

6. My name makes me sound like something you would see in the sky, but the place to find me is at the beach. I am a ___starfish___ .

Copyright © Houghton Mifflin Company. All rights reserved. **Use with text pages 240–242.**

Divide Greater Numbers

Read the meanings of these terms.

up to 10 years old	ten years old or less
at least 10 years old	10 years old or more
twice the age	the age multiplied by 2
4 times the age	the age multiplied by 4
half the age	the age divided by 2
6 years older than	the age plus 6

Complete the sentences about the children.
Use the words in bold type above.

1. Anthony is 5. Bakari is 11.

   Bakari is __6 years older than__ Anthony.

2. Carla is 12. Debra is 6.

   Debra is __half the age__ of Carla.

3. Erric is 8. Fred is 10.

   They could play on a team for boys
   __up to ten years old__.

4. Galya is 3. Hal is 12.

   Hal is __4 times the age__ of Gayla.

5. Ingrid is 10. Lynn is 13.

   They could play on a team for girls
   __at least 10 years old__.

6. Kyle is 7. Luisa is 14.

   Luisa is __twice the age__ of Kyle.

Copyright © Houghton Mifflin Company. All rights reserved.

Use with text pages 244–246.

Factors and Multiples

Read these explanations.

> The general meaning of **multiple** is "having more than one of something." The specific math meaning of **multiple** is "a number that another number can be divided into, leaving no remainder."
>
> The general meaning of **factor** is "something that helps bring about a certain result." The specific math meaning of **factor** is "one of two or more numbers that can be multiplied to make a certain product."

Circle *general* or *specific to math* to tell how *multiple* or *factor* is used in each sentence.

1. Dry weather was a **factor** in the death of 16 of the 50 corn plants in Lee's backyard.

   general   specific to math

2. The car cost $456 to fix because it had **multiple** problems.

   general   specific to math

3. Val wanted to find out if 11 was a **factor** of 176.

   general   specific to math

4. Dino made **multiple** copies of a 10-page story he wrote.

   general   specific to math

5. Frieda knew that since 20 is a **multiple** of 4, she could divide 20 stickers evenly among 4 friends.

   general   specific to math

6. Mimi thought 7 was a **factor** of 27, but when she looked at the 7 row on the multiplication chart, she did not see 27.

   general   specific to math

Copyright © Houghton Mifflin Company. All rights reserved.

Use with text pages 252–253.

Prime and Composite Numbers

Read these definitions.

compose	to create by putting together
composite	made up of different parts
composite number	a number that has more than two factors
prime	first in quality or importance
primary	the earliest; the most basic
prime number	a number that has only 2 factors—1 and itself

Use terms from the box to complete the sentences.

compose	**composite**	**composite number**
prime	**primary**	**prime number**

1. Red, blue, and yellow are the ___*primary*___ colors. You can use them to make all the other colors.

2. Melanie will use pictures, objects, and drawings to ___*compose*___ a display. It will be made of many different things.

3. The number 18 is a ___*composite number*___ because it has 1, 2, 3, 6, and 9 as factors.

4. A ___*prime*___ minister is the most important of all the ministers in a government.

5. Bip has tried to divide 41 by many numbers, but every one leaves a remainder. He has decided that 41 must be a ___*prime number*___.

6. Edwin made a ___*composite*___ face by cutting up several photos of faces and putting together parts from each.

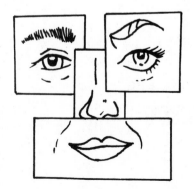

Copyright © Houghton Mifflin Company. All rights reserved.

Use with text pages 254–256.

Problem-Solving Strategy:
Solve a Simpler Problem

Read each definition.

row of boxes	boxes put beside each other in a line
animal pen	fenced area to keep animals in
end to end	objects lined up the long way in a single row
relay race	race in which each team member runs one part of the race
maximum temperature	the hottest temperature

Circle your answers.

1. Which is a **relay race**?

   Rula raced against Sue. Rula won.

   Ali, Laura, Risa, and Sheva each ran 1 lap in the race. They beat the team of Erica, Molly, Diane, and LaVonne.

2. Which is a **row of boxes**?

3. Which thermometer shows the **maximum temperature** displayed?

   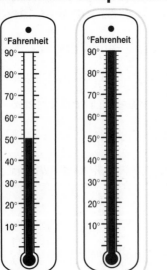

4. Which sheep are in an **animal pen**?

5. Which dominoes are laid **end to end**?

   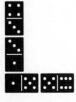

Copyright © Houghton Mifflin Company. All rights reserved.

Use with text pages 258–260.

Model Mean

**Read this problem. Study the number sentences that show
how to solve it.**

> Lem scored 7 points in the first game, 4 points in the second game,
> and 1 point in the third game. What was his mean score?
>
> $$7 + 4 + 1 = 12$$
>
> $$12 \div 3 = 4$$

**Use words from the box to complete the explanation of
how to solve this kind of problem. (You will only use some
of the words.)**

subtract	each	highest	multiply	add
one	divide	equal	mean	odd

1. First you need to know how many points the player scored in ___each___ game.

2. Then you ___add___ the scores.

3. After that, you ___divide___ the total by the number of games played.

4. The answer tells you the player's ___mean___ score.

5. Finding an average is the same as gathering together some items and then dividing

   them into ___equal___ groups.

Copyright © Houghton Mifflin Company. All rights reserved.

Use with text pages 262–263.

Name _____   Date _____

Find the Mean

Read Jim Ray's explanation of how he picked 3 numbers that have a mean of 50.

Three numbers with a mean of 50 must equal 3 × 50.
3 × 50 = 150. So, I needed to pick 3 numbers that add up to 150.

The first number could be any number from 0 to 150. I picked 21.
150 − 21 is 129. I needed to pick 2 numbers that add up to 129.

The second number could be any number from 0 to 129. I picked
88. 129 − 88 = 41. My last number had to be 41. 21, 88, and 41
add up to 150. 150 ÷ 3 = 50.

Fill in the blanks below. Complete the explanation of how to find 3 numbers that have a mean of 121.

Three numbers with a mean of 121 must equal 3 × ___121___.

3 × ___121___ = ___363___. So, I needed to pick 3 numbers that add up

to ___363___.

The first number could be any number from 0 to ___363___. I picked _____ *.

___363___ − _____ * is _____ ** . I needed to pick 2 numbers that add up

to _____ ** .

The second number could be any number from 0 to _____ ** . I picked _____ *** .

_____ ** − _____ *** = _____ **** . My last number had to be _____ **** .

_____ *, _____ *** , and _____ **** add up to ___363___.

___363___ ÷ 3 = ___121___. *Number picked will vary but
should be less than 363.
**This number is the difference between 363
and *.
***Number picked will vary but should be less
than **.
****The last number must be the difference
between ** and ***.

Copyright © Houghton Mifflin Company. All rights reserved.

Use with text pages 264–266.

Divide by Multiples of 10

Look at these standings. They tell how four teams finished
in a baseball league last year.

Standings
First: Ducks
Second: Hawks
Third: Crows
Fourth: Robins

Write *ahead of* or *after* to make each sentence tell about
how the teams finished.

1. The Crows finished _____after_____ the Hawks.

2. The Hawks finished _____ahead of_____ the Robins.

3. The Robins finished _____after_____ the Ducks.

4. The Ducks finished _____ahead of_____ the Crows.

5. The Hawks finished _____after_____ the Ducks.

6. The Crows finished _____ahead of_____ the Robins.

These sentences tell about how the same teams finished
this year. Read the sentences. Then list how the teams
finished.

The Robins finished ahead of the Ducks.

The Robins finished after the Hawks.

The Crows finished ahead of the Hawks.

Standings

First: _____Crows_____

Second: _____Hawks_____

Third: _____Robins_____

Fourth: _____Ducks_____

Copyright © Houghton Mifflin Company. All rights reserved.

Use with text pages 272–273.

Estimate Quotients

Read these definitions.

trash	things no one wants
collect	to gather
recycle	to reuse material in things that would otherwise be put into a dump
volunteer	someone who agrees to work for no pay
cleanup	a project in which people gather and get rid of trash

Use each word in bold type above to complete the sentences below.

1. The families on Craig's block want to make their area look nicer. That is why they

   have decided to hold a neighborhood _____cleanup_____.

2. Mary was a _____volunteer_____ on cleanup day last year. She was happy to
   work for free. This year she has asked her friend Evan to help with the cleanup.

3. There are some old buildings on the block that have a lot of

   _____trash_____ in their yards.

4. Evan and Mary have pairs of heavy gloves to wear on their hands. They will wear

   these gloves when they _____collect_____ this trash and put it in bags.

5. The volunteers know that old paper can be made into new paper. So, instead of

   putting paper in the trash bags, they will _____recycle_____ it.

Copyright © Houghton Mifflin Company. All rights reserved.

Use with text pages 274–275.

Model Division by Two-Digit Divisors

This diagram shows the **eruption** of a geyser. The geyser **erupts** many times each day.

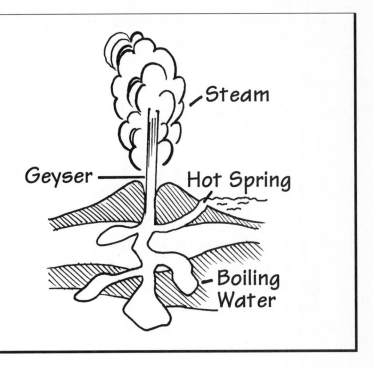

Steam

Geyser

Hot Spring

Boiling
Water

Use words from the box to complete these sentences.

| steam | boiling water | geyser | eruption | hot spring | erupts |

1. Hot water that comes out of the ground is called a _____hot spring_____.

2. A hot spring that erupts is called a _____geyser_____.

3. When a geyser erupts, it sends _____boiling water_____ and _____steam_____ into the air.

4. When a geyser shoots hot water into the air, the event is called an _____eruption_____.

5. When a geyser _____erupts_____, a person standing too close could get burned.

Copyright © Houghton Mifflin Company. All rights reserved.

Use with text pages 276–278.

One-Digit Quotients

Read this information. Look at the examples.

When you divide by a two-digit divisor, you begin by **estimating** the quotient. Estimating helps you know where to place the first digit of the quotient.

To estimate a quotient of a problem with a two-digit divisor, you must compare the divisor to the first two digits of the dividend.

 17)81

Here, the divisor is **less than** the first two digits of the dividend.

22)167

Here, the divisor is **more than** the first two digits of the dividend.

If the two-digit divisor is **less than** the first two digits in the dividend, the first digit of the quotient goes above the second digit in the dividend.

☐
17)81 ◄── | first digit in quotient goes here |

If the two-digit divisor is **more than** the first two digits in the dividend, the first digit of the quotient goes above the third digit in the dividend.

☐
22)167 ◄── | first digit in quotient goes here |

In each problem below, compare the division to the first two digits in the dividend. Write **more than** or **less than** in the blank.

1. 31)95 The divisor is __less than__ the first two digits of the dividend.

2. 62)240 The divisor is __more than__ the first two digits of the dividend.

3. 79)625 The divisor is __more than__ the first two digits of the dividend.

4. 56)65 The divisor is __less than__ the first two digits of the dividend.

5. 26)187 The divisor is __more than__ the first two digits of the dividend.

Copyright © Houghton Mifflin Company. All rights reserved.

Use with text pages 280–281.

Two-Digit Quotients

Read this explanation.

An **advantage** is something that helps you do better. If you have an **advantage,** it's easier for you to be successful. A **disadvantage** is something that makes it harder for you to do well. If you have a **disadvantage,** it is harder for you to be successful than it is for others.

The prefix *dis-* usually means "the opposite of."

Write *advantage* or *disadvantage* after each item.

1. You run in a race. One shoelace comes untied. disadvantage

2. You play a quiz game. All the questions are about your favorite sport. advantage

3. You enter a cooking contest. The food you cook is a food you have made many times. advantage

4. You enter a swimming race. You get a late start. disadvantage

Read the explanation. Then write a definition.

5. **Connect** means "put things together."

 Disconnect means "take things apart".

Copyright © Houghton Mifflin Company. All rights reserved.

Use with text pages 282–285.

Adjust the Quotient

Read this passage.

Tolia and his friends made a **time capsule.** They found a steel box, a container that would last a long time. They filled this container with things that showed what their lives were like. Tolia put in a **video** that showed him playing soccer with his brother. His friend Calvin put in an **audiotape.** It was a **recorded message** from his father telling about the family's barber shop. Tolia's cousin Corrina put in an **essay** about why friends are important. She had written the essay the week before. After the friends filled the box, they dug a hole and buried it. "Someday someone will dig this up," said Tolia. "They can find out about us by watching, listening, and reading."

Think about making your own time capsule. Then answer these questions by finishing the sentences.

1–5: Accept all reasonable responses.

1. What would you use for a time capsule?

   I would use _____.

2. What would you use a video to show?

   On my video, I would show _____.

3. What would you record on an audiotape?

   I would record _____.

4. What other recorded message would you put in?

   I would put in a message that told about _____.

5. What would you write an essay about for your time capsule?

   I would write an essay about _____.

Copyright © Houghton Mifflin Company. All rights reserved.

Use with text pages 286–287.

Name _____ Date _____

Problem-Solving Decision: Multistep Problems

Look at the words and phrases in this picture dictionary.

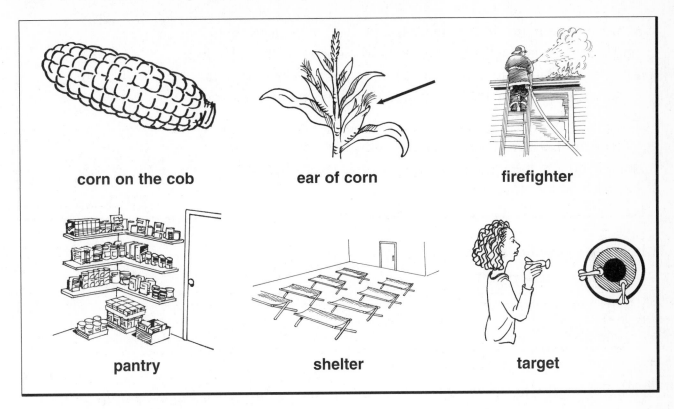

corn on the cob   ear of corn   firefighter

pantry   shelter   target

Use the words and phrases to solve these riddles.

1. You want to hit the center of this.

   target

2. You want to put butter on this and eat it.

   corn on the cob

3. You could sleep here to stay out of a storm.

   shelter

4. You could find many things to eat in here.

   pantry

5. You should call this kind of person if you see something burning.

   firefighter

6. You want to pick this and pull the leaves off, so you can cook it and eat it.

   ear of corn

Copyright © Houghton Mifflin Company. All rights reserved.

Use with text page 288.

Name _____ Date _____

Explore Customary Units of Length

Read these explanations.

When you **measure to the nearest inch,** you measure something and then give its length as the closest whole inch on the ruler. If a bean is a little more than 5 inches long, you give its length as 5 inches. If a bean is a little less than 6 inches, you give its length as 6 inches.

When you **measure to the nearest half-inch,** you measure something and then give its length as the closest whole inch or half-inch on the ruler.

Circle the correct answers.

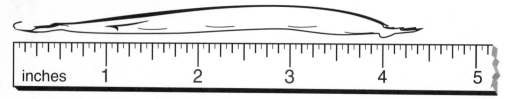

1. You measure this bean to the nearest inch. What is its length?

   A. $3\frac{1}{2}$ inches   **B.** 4 inches

   C. $4\frac{1}{2}$ inches   **D.** 5 inches

2. You measure the same bean to the nearest half-inch. What is its length?

   A. $3\frac{1}{2}$ inches   **B.** 4 inches

   C. $4\frac{1}{2}$ inches   **D.** 5 inches

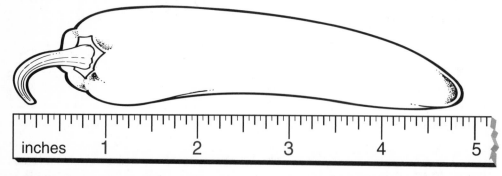

3. You measure this pepper to the nearest inch. What is its length?

   A. 4 inches   **B.** $4\frac{1}{2}$ inches

   C. 5 inches   **D.** 6 inches

4. You measure the same pepper to the nearest half-inch. What is its length?

   A. $4\frac{1}{2}$ inches   **B.** 5 inches

   C. $5\frac{1}{2}$ inches   **D.** 6 inches

Copyright © Houghton Mifflin Company. All rights reserved.

Use with text pages 306–307.

Inch, Foot, Yard, Mile

Read this explanation.

An **adjective** is a word that describes. In English, many adjectives add -*er* to compare two things.

> Nelly has a **long** rope.
> It is **longer** than Edwina's rope.

These adjectives add -*est* to compare more than two things.

> Talia's rope is longer than Nelly's. It is the **longest** of all.

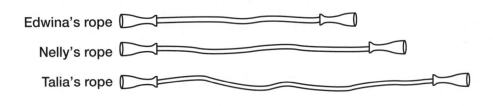

Edwina's rope
Nelly's rope
Talia's rope

Read this information. Then write *longer, longest, shorter,* **or** *shortest* **to complete each sentence.**

Wire <u>A</u> is one inch long.

Wire <u>B</u> is one foot long.

Wire <u>C</u> is one yard long.

Wire <u>D</u> is one mile long.

> 12 inches = 1 foot
>
> 3 feet = 1 yard
>
> 1760 yards = 1 mile

1. Wire <u>A</u> is _____shorter_____ than wire <u>B</u>.

2. Wire <u>D</u> is _____longer_____ than wire <u>B</u>.

3. Wire <u>B</u> is _____shorter_____ than wire <u>C</u>.

4. Wire <u>C</u> is _____longer_____ than wire <u>A</u>.

5. Wire <u>A</u> is _____shortest_____ of all.

6. Wire <u>D</u> is _____longest_____ of all.

Copyright © Houghton Mifflin Company. All rights reserved.

Customary Units of Capacity

Read these definitions.

customary	commonly used
capacity	the amount something can hold
container	something made to hold other things
watering can	a container with a spout, used to give water to plants
recipe	instructions for preparing a type of food
measuring cup	a container used to find exact amounts of ingredients for recipes

Write answers on the lines after the questions.

1. Would you follow a **recipe** to make a soup, or to make a puppet?   to make a soup

2. Which is a **container,** a box or a board?   a box

3. Which is a **customary** unit of capacity, a quart or a quack?   a quart

4. If you were making a cake, would you use a **measuring cup** or a **watering can**?   measuring cup

5. Does **capacity** tell how long something will last, or how much it will hold?   how much it will hold

6. Does **customary** mean "usual" or "unusual"?   "usual"

7. Would you use a **watering can** to wash windows, or help flowers in containers grow?   help flowers in containers grow

8. Is the **capacity** of a quart of milk "one quart," or "some milk"?   one quart

Copyright © Houghton Mifflin Company. All rights reserved.

Use with text pages 310–311.

Customary Units of Weight

Look at the pictures. Read the explanation.

strawberries

handful

blueberries

classroom

watermelon

Each word above is a **compound word**—a word made up of two smaller words. Sometimes thinking about the meanings of the smaller words can help you figure out the meaning of the compound word.

Match each word with its definition.

1. blueberries   "sweet red berries"

2. classroom   "a juicy melon that is green on the outside and red on the inside"

3. watermelon   "berries that are a shade of blue"

4. strawberries   "an amount that fills up one hand"

5. handful   "a room where class is held"

In each sentence below, there is a mixed-up compound word. Cross it out. Write the correct word on the line.

6. We go to a ~~classmelon~~ to learn about math.   classroom _____

7. The top of the cake was blue because it was covered with ~~handberries~~.   blueberries _____

8. The best food at the picnic was the big green ~~waterful~~.   watermelon _____

Copyright © Houghton Mifflin Company. All rights reserved.

Use with text pages 312–314.

Too Much or Too Little Information

Read this paragraph.

Lisa works in the school garden. She is planting four kinds of flowers. Three grow from **bulbs.** These are **tulips, lilies,** and **crocuses.** She is also planting **marigolds,** which grow from **seeds.** The seeds come in paper envelopes called **seed packets.** Lisa will plant the bulbs in the ground. Later she will put **fertilizer** where she planted the bulbs, to help the plants grow. She will plant the marigold seeds in **pots.** The young plants will be safe from bugs and snails in the pots.

Tulip bulb

Tulips

Use words from the box to complete the sentences.

tulips	lilies	crocuses	seed packets
bulbs	fertilizer	pots	marigolds

1. If you want a young plant to grow, you can use _____.

   (The order may differ.)

2. Three kinds of flowers that grow from bulbs are _____,
   _____, and _____.

3. Round containers for growing flowers are called _____.

4. If you want to plant marigolds, you should buy _____.

5. If you want to grow tulips, you should buy _____.

6. _____ are flowers that grow from seeds.

Copyright © Houghton Mifflin Company. All rights reserved.

Use with text page 316.

Name _____   Date _____

Explore Metric Units of Length

Read this explanation.

The prefix *centi-* means "100."

There are 100 centimeters in a meter.

The prefix *milli-* means "1,000."

There are 1,000 millimeters in a meter.

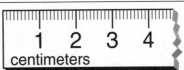

The numbered marks show centimeters.
The tiny lines between centimeters show millimeters.

Look at the prefix of each word in bold type. Think about its meaning. Then write your answer on the line.

1. Is a **millennium** 100 or 1,000 years?

   _____1,000 years_____

2. Are there 100 **centigrams** or 1,000 **centigrams** in a gram?

   _____100 centigrams_____

3. Are there 100 **milliliters** or 1,000 **milliliters** in a liter?

   _____1,000 milliliters_____

4. Is a **century** 100 years or 1,000 years?

   _____100 years_____

5. A **centipede** is a bug with many legs and feet. Does it have about 100 legs and feet, or about 1,000 legs and feet?

   _____about 100 legs and feet_____

6. Are there 100 or 1,000 **milliseconds** in a second?

   _____1,000 milliseconds_____

Copyright © Houghton Mifflin Company. All rights reserved.

Use with text pages 318–319.

Metric Units of Length

Read this explanation.

Length is the distance from one end of something to the other end. **Length** is the measure of the **long** part of something.

Width is the distance across something. **Width** is the measure of how **wide** something is.

Longer is a word used to compare the lengths of two things. **Longest** is a word used to compare the lengths of more than two things.

Wider is a word used to compare the widths of two things. **Widest** is a word used to compare the widths of more than two things.

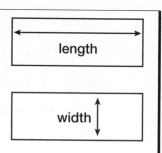

Look at the diagrams.

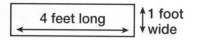

4 feet long   ↑1 foot ↓ wide

Curt's Table

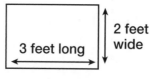

3 feet long   2 feet wide

Rula's Table

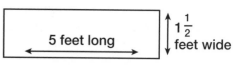

5 feet long $1\frac{1}{2}$ feet wide

Fumi's Table

Write sentences to answer these questions.

1. What is the width of Curt's table?

   Curt's table is 1 foot wide. (or) The width of Curt's table is 1 foot.

2. What is the length of Fumi's table?

   Fumi's table is 5 feet long. (or) The length of Fumi's table is 5 feet.

3. Whose table is wider than Fumi's table?

   Rula's table is wider than Fumi's table.

4. Whose table is longer than Curt's table?

   Fumi's table is longer than Curt's table.

5. Whose table is the longest?

   Fumi's table is the longest.

6. Whose table is the widest?

   Rula's table is the widest.

Copyright © Houghton Mifflin Company. All rights reserved.

Use with text pages 320–321.

Metric Units of Capacity

Look at the drawings.

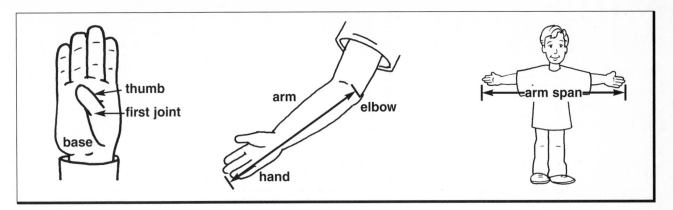

Answer the questions.

1. Which is longer, the length of the first joint of the thumb or the distance from elbow to hand?

   <u>the distance from elbow to hand</u>

2. Which is shorter, the distance from elbow to hand or the arm span?

   <u>the distance from elbow to hand</u>

3. Which is the shortest, the length of the first joint of the thumb, the distance from elbow to hand, or the arm span?

   <u>the length of the first joint of the thumb</u>

4. Which is the longest, the length of the first joint of the thumb, the distance from elbow to hand, or the arm span?

   <u>the arm span</u>

5. Each drawing at the top of the page shows a personal benchmark—a length having to do with a part of your body. Think of another personal benchmark you could use. Draw a picture of it. Then write what it is.

Answers
will vary.

_____
_____
_____
_____

Copyright © Houghton Mifflin Company. All rights reserved.

Explore Metric Units of Mass

Look at the pictures and read the labels.

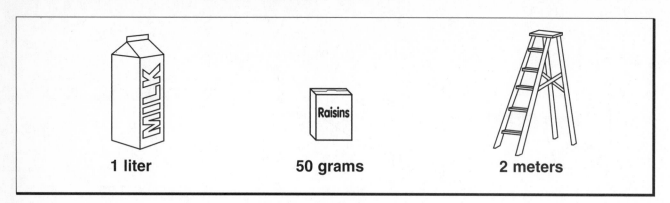

| 1 liter | 50 grams | 2 meters |

Write each term from the box in the correct place in the chart. The pictures above can help you.

kilometer	decimeter	centimeter
gram	kilogram	liter
milliliter	meter	millimeter

3–7: The lengths may appear in any order.

Mass	**Length**	**Capacity**
1. ___gram___	3. ___kilometer___	8. ___milliliter___
2. ___kilogram___	4. ___decimeter___	9. ___liter___
1–2: The masses may appear in any order.	5. ___meter___	8–9: The capacities may appear in any order.
	6. ___centimeter___	
	7. ___millimeter___	

Underline the correct answers.

10. A liter is (<u>more</u>, less) than a milliliter.

11. A gram is (more, <u>less</u>) than a kilogram.

12. A decimeter is (shorter, <u>longer</u>) than a centimeter.

Copyright © Houghton Mifflin Company. All rights reserved.

Use with text pages 326–328.

Calendar

Read the definitions. They tell how the listed words are
used in Lesson 1.

elapsed time	the amount of time between two days or events
day	day of the week; for example, Monday
date	a day's number, month, and year; for example, June 15, 2004
century	100 years
decade	10 years
leap year	a year that has 366 days instead of 365
series	a set of events, talks, or performances

Fill in the blanks below to complete the sentences. Use the
words in the box to do this.

elapsed time	**day**	**date**	**century**
decade	**leap year**	**series**	

1. Every four years a day is added to the year. A year with a day added is called

   a __leap year__.

2. July 4, 1776 was the _____date_____ on which the United States of America
   became a nation.

3. Ruben wants to see all 5 plays that the local theater group will perform this year,

   so he has bought tickets for the whole _____series_____.

4. If you swim in a race, a coach may watch to see how much time it takes you to

   complete the race. The coach will then write down this _____elapsed time_____ on a chart.

5. Friday is the _____day_____ that comes after Thursday.

6. The period from January 1, 1991 to December 31, 2000 was a _____decade_____.

7. The period from January 1, 2001 to December 31, 2100 will be a _____century_____.

Copyright © Houghton Mifflin Company. All rights reserved.

Use with text pages 334–335.

Elapsed Time

Read this paragraph. Pay attention to the words in bold type.

Linda wants to take a tour of the local doll factory. Tours begin **every 20 minutes.** She wants to go on either the 9:00 tour, the 9:20 tour, or the 9:40 tour. The tours **last** for 55 minutes. If Linda arrives **in time** to take the 9:00 tour, she will be finished at 9:55, or 5 minutes to 10. Saying "9:55" is expressing the time as **time after the hour.** Saying "5 minutes to 10" is expressing the time as **time before the hour.** Linda needs to be home by **half-past eleven,** because she has a music lesson ten minutes later, at 11:40.

DOLL FACTORY MORNING TOURS		
9:00	10:00	11:00
9:20	10:20	11:20
9:40	10:40	11:40

Draw lines to match the terms with the meanings they have in the paragraph above.

1. every 20 minutes   "soon enough to do something"

2. last   "11:40"

3. in time   "with 20 minutes of time elapsing between an event and the next one"

4. time after the hour   "have an elapsed time of"

5. time before the hour   "11:30"

6. half-past eleven   "20 minutes to 12"

Copyright © Houghton Mifflin Company. All rights reserved.

Use with text pages 336–338.

Guess and Check

Study the pictures.

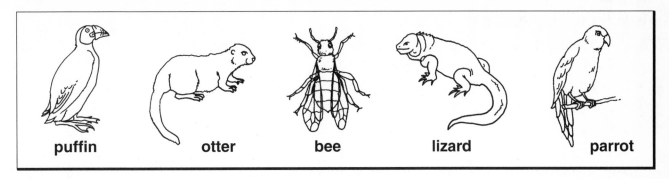

| puffin | otter | bee | lizard | parrot |

Tell how many legs each creature has.

1. puffin = __2__ legs
2. bee = __6__ legs
3. parrot = __2__ legs
4. otter = __4__ legs
5. lizard = __4__ legs

Look at each picture. In the sentence below it, fill the blanks with the correct numbers.

6.

This picture shows __3__ animals with __8__ legs.

7.

This picture shows __4__ animals with __14__ legs.

8.

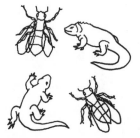

This picture shows __4__ animals with __20__ legs.

9.

This picture shows __5__ animals with __14__ legs.

Copyright © Houghton Mifflin Company. All rights reserved.

Use with text pages 340–342.

Temperature and Negative Numbers

Read these explanations.

vertical	up-and-down
negative	less than zero or below zero
positive	greater than zero or above zero
room temperature	the usual temperature inside a home
gradually	in a steady manner
normal body temperature	the temperature of a healthy person
degrees centigrade	temperature on a scale on which water freezes at 0° and boils at 100°
degrees Fahrenheit	temperature on a scale on which water freezes at 32° and boils at 212°

°Celsius   °Fahrenheit

Use the bold terms above to fill the blanks.

1. If you save $2 each week to buy skates, you save money ____gradually____.

2. If you put a thermometer in ice water and it shows a temperature of about zero, it is showing temperature in ____degrees centigrade____.

3. If you jump up, you make a ____vertical____ movement.

4. Most people have a ____normal body temperature____ of about 98.6°F.

5. If you put a thermometer in ice water and it shows a temperature of about 32°, it is showing temperatures in ____degrees Fahrenheit____.

6. The normal temperature inside a house is ____room temperature____.

7. If a temperature is below zero, it is a ____negative____ temperature.

8. If a temperature is above zero, it is a ____positive____ temperature.

Copyright © Houghton Mifflin Company. All rights reserved.

Use with text pages 344–346.

Use Temperature

Read these rules.

Some verbs add *-ed* to talk about the past.
My friends **climb** icy hills. → Yesterday Chico **climbed** a
very steep hill. → He **has climbed** all the hills in our area.

Some verbs change form to talk about the past.
The temperature **rises** when the sun comes out. →
Yesterday it **rose** 10° in two hours. → Today the
temperature **has risen** 6° since the sun came out.

The temperature **falls** when the sun goes down. →
Yesterday it **fell** 8° during the hour after sunset. →
Tonight the temperature **has fallen** 5° in the last hour.

Draw a line under the correct verb.

1. Arlette (clumb, climbed) an icy peak last Thursday.

2. She has (climb, climbed) Mount Washington.

3. Yesterday the sun (rised, rose) at 6 A.M.

4. Dark clouds filled the sky, and the temperature (fell, falled) quickly.

5. The temperature has (rised, risen) 5° since noon today.

6. A tree has (falled, fallen) in our backyard.

7. The temperature inside our home (rose, rised) quickly after Luke turned on the heat.

8. My grandmother called and told us the temperature in her area had (fallen, falled) to ⁻5°F.

Copyright © Houghton Mifflin Company. All rights reserved.

Use with text pages 348–350.

Name _____ Date _____

Collect and Organize Data

Read these definitions.

from least to greatest	from lowest amount to highest amount
from most to least popular	in order, from the one liked by the most people to the one liked by the fewest people
two most popular	the one liked by the most people and the one liked by the second most people
combined	put together

Look at the tally chart. Circle your answers.

What Is Your Favorite Local News Show?	
Littletown News	|||
Big Stories from Littletown	||||		
Hometown Headlines	||||

1. Which are the **two most popular** shows?
   A. Littletown News and Big Stories from Littletown
   B. Littletown News and Hometown Headlines
   (C.) Big Stories from Littletown and Hometown Headlines

2. How many people **combined** chose Big Stories from Littletown and Hometown Headlines?
   A. 4   B. 7   (C.) 10   D. 13

3. Which list gives the shows in order, **from most to least popular**?

   <u>List A</u>   (<u>List B</u>)
   Littletown News   Big Stories from Littletown
   Hometown Headlines   Hometown Headlines
   Big Stories from Littletown   Littletown News

4. Which list shows the number of votes in order, **from least to greatest**?
   A. 6, 4, 3   B. 4, 3, 6   C. 6, 3, 4   (D.) 3, 4, 6

Copyright © Houghton Mifflin Company. All rights reserved.

Use with text pages 356–358.

Make a Table

Read each sentence. Then read the paraphrase, which says the same thing in a different way.

Original Sentence	Paraphrase
Art is twice Bob's age.	Art's age ÷ 2 = Bob's age OR Bob's age × 2 = Art's age
Cal is half Dee's age.	Cal's age × 2 = Dee's age OR Dee's age ÷ 2 = Cal's age
A plant doubles its height each week.	plant's height on one day × 2 = plant's height 7 days later
Each person is 3 inches taller than the next tallest person.	first person's height + 3″ = second person's height second person's height + 3″ = third person's height

Circle the correct example.

1. Emma is half Fran's age.
   A. Emma is 20. Fran is 30.
   B. Emma is 40. Fran is 20.
   C. Emma is 40. Fran is 80.

2. Gus is twice Haruo's age.
   A. Gus is 6. Haruo is 12.
   B. Gus is 3. Haruo is 12.
   C. Gus is 6. Haruo is 3.

3. A plant doubles its height every week.
   A. Week 1: 2″. Week 2: 4″. Week 3: 8″.
   B. Week 1: 2″. Week 2: 3″. Week 3: 4″.
   C. Week 1: 2″. Week 2: 4″. Week 3: 6″.

4. Each person is 3 inches taller than the next tallest person.
   A. 5′1″, 8′1″, 11′1″
   B. 5′1″, 5′3″, 5′6″
   C. 5′1″, 5′4″, 5′7″

Copyright © Houghton Mifflin Company. All rights reserved.

Use with text pages 360–362.

Mean, Median, Mode, and Range

Read the explanations.

The **mean** of a group of numbers can also be called the average of those numbers. To find the mean, you add all the numbers together. Then you divide the sum by the number of addends.

The **median** is the number in the middle of a group of numbers that have been put in order.

The **mode** is the number that appears most often in a group of numbers.

The **range** is the difference between the **largest** number and the **smallest** number in a group of numbers.

- The largest number is also called the **greatest** number.
- The smallest number is also called the **least** number.

Answer the questions for each group of numbers.

9, 7, 6, 6, 2

1. Which number is in the middle of these numbers? ___6___

2. What is the median of this group of numbers? ___6___

3. To find the mean, what numbers would you add? ___$9 + 7 + 6 + 6 + 2$___

4. What number would you divide by? ___5___

5. What number appears most often in this group of numbers? ___6___

6. What is the mode of this group of numbers? ___6___

9, 7, 4, 2

7. Which is the greatest number? ___9___

8. Which is the least number? ___2___

9. What can you find by subtracting the least number from the greatest number? ___the range___

Copyright © Houghton Mifflin Company. All rights reserved.

Use with text pages 364–365.

Line Plots

Read this comic strip.

Use this display to answer the questions below.

1. What is the name of this way of showing data? Circle your answer.
   A. a tally sheet
   B. a line plot
   C. a line graph
   D. a pie chart

   Number of Cats at Home

   ```
              X
    X    X    X              X
   ────────────────────────────
    0    1    2    3    4
   ```

2. How many people were surveyed? ___5___

3. How many people said they had no cats at home? ___1___

4. What response was given most often? ___1___ cat

5. How many people said they had 4 cats? ___1___

Copyright © Houghton Mifflin Company. All rights reserved.

Use with text pages 366–368.

Stem-and-Leaf Plots

Read the information.

This is a plant.
The thick part is
its stem. 3 leaves
are attached to
the stem.

This chart shows
how many dishes
Sal washed on
5 days. He will
make a stem-
and-leaf plot of
the data.

The digits in the
tens column will
be the stems. The
digits in the ones
column will be
the leaves.

Stem	Leaf
2	1 5 7
3	4
6	2

Three numbers on
the chart have the
same stem—2. That
stem has 3 leaves—
the ones digits in
21, 25, and 27. The
other stems each
have only 1 leaf.

Read the sentences below. Answer these questions.

Sal washed 41 dishes on Saturday. He wants to add this information to the
stem-and-leaf plot.

1. What number is the stem? ___4___

2. What number is the leaf? ___1___

Sal washed 22 dishes on Sunday. He wants to add this information to the
stem-and-leaf plot, too.

3. Does he need to add a stem to the plot? __no__

4. Does he need to add a leaf to the plot? __yes__

An **outlier** is a value that is much less or much more than the other values.

5. Is there a value in Sal's stem-and-leaf plot that is much greater than any

   other value? __yes__

6. Is there a value in Sal's stem-and-leaf plot that is much less than any

   other value? __no__

7. What number in his stem-and-leaf plot is the **outlier**? __62__

Copyright © Houghton Mifflin Company. All rights reserved. **Use with text pages 370–371.**

Name _____ Date _____

Double Bar Graphs

Look at the items below. Read the labels in bold type.

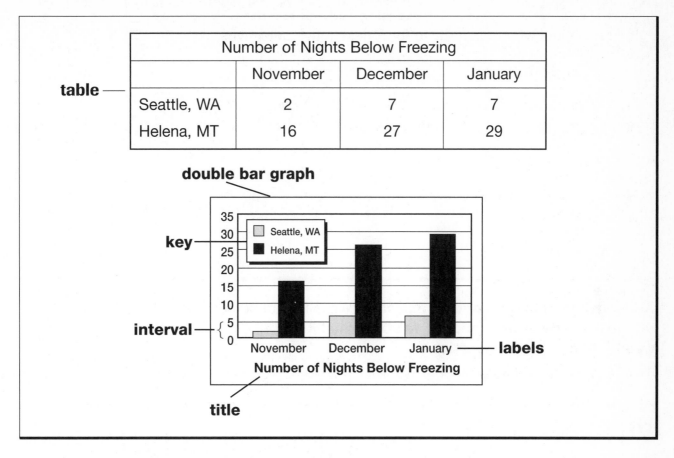

table

Number of Nights Below Freezing			
	November	December	January
Seattle, WA	2	7	7
Helena, MT	16	27	29

double bar graph

key

Seattle, WA
Helena, MT

interval

November   December   January — **labels**

Number of Nights Below Freezing

title

Answer these questions. Use the labels in bold type.

1. What part of the graph tells you what city each bar stands for? _____ *key* _____

2. What part of the graph tells you the month that each pair of bars gives data about? _____ *labels* _____

3. What is the name for a chart that has rows and columns of numbers? _____ *table* _____

4. What is the name for a graph that compares two sets of data using bars? _____ *double bar graph* _____

5. What is the name for the difference between pairs of numbers on the side of the graph? _____ *interval* _____

6. What tells what kind of information the graph presents? _____ *title* _____

Copyright © Houghton Mifflin Company. All rights reserved.

Use with text pages 376–377.

Name _____ Date _____

Circle Graphs

Read this explanation.

In English, many nouns add *y* to form descriptive adjectives.

rain → rain**y**

Nouns that end with a short vowel sound and a consonant double the consonant when adding *y*.

sun → sun**ny**

Nouns that have a long vowel sound and a silent *e* drop the *e* when adding *y*.

breez**e** → breez**y**

Add *y* to each noun to form an adjective. Write the adjective on the line. Then draw a picture to show what kind of weather the adjective describes.

1. snow __*snowy*__   **2.** cloud __*cloudy*__   **3.** storm __*stormy*__

Students' drawings should reflect an understanding of these adjectives.

4. fog __*foggy*__   **5.** haze __*hazy*__   **6.** wind __*windy*__

Copyright © Houghton Mifflin Company. All rights reserved.

Use with text pages 378–379.

Interpret a Line Graph

Read this information.

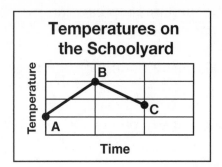

This graph shows how the temperature changed on the schoolyard during one day at Park School. The higher a dot is, the higher the temperature.

Look at this graph. Tell whether each statement is true or false by circling the correct answer.

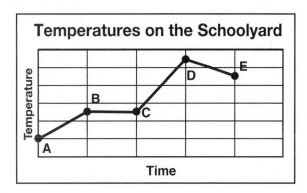

1. This graph shows exact temperatures.   True   (False)

2. A line rising upward means the temperature was getting warmer.   (True)   False

3. The temperature rose between Time *A* and Time *B*.   (True)   False

4. The temperature fell between Time *D* and Time *E*.   (True)   False

5. The temperature stayed the same between Time *C* and Time *D*.   True   (False)

6. The highest temperature shown is the temperature at Time *D*.   (True)   False

7. The lowest temperature shown is the temperature at Time *E*.   True   (False)

8. The temperature stayed the same between Time *B* and Time *C*.   (True)   False

Copyright © Houghton Mifflin Company. All rights reserved.

Use with text pages 380–381.

Read and Make Line Graphs

Read these explanations.

> An **axis** of a graph shows the amounts represented by the lines in the graph.
>
> The **horizontal** axis is the axis at the bottom of the graph. It runs sideways.
>
> The **vertical** axis is the axis at the left side of the graph. It runs up and down.
>
> **Depth** is the measure of how deep something is.

Look at this line graph. Circle the correct answers.

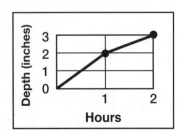

1. What does the horizontal axis show?

how many hours have passed   how deep the snow is

2. What does the vertical axis show?

how many hours have passed   how deep the snow is

3. What do the larger numbers on the vertical axis show?

more snow   less snow

4. What do the larger numbers on the horizontal axis show?

more time   less time

5. What does the line on this graph show?

the depth of snow going up   the depth of snow going down

Copyright © Houghton Mifflin Company. All rights reserved.

Use with text pages 382–383.

Analyze Graphs

Look at the four graphs below.

Best Place to Hike

Hill Trail
Valley Trail
Meadow Trail
Canyon Trail

= 2 votes

Pictograph

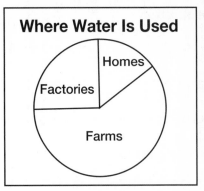

Where Water Is Used

Homes
Factories
Farms

Circle Graph

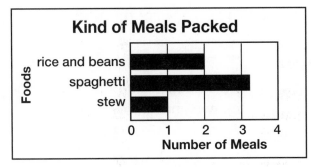

Kind of Meals Packed

Foods
rice and beans
spaghetti
stew

0   1   2   3   4
Number of Meals

Bar Graph

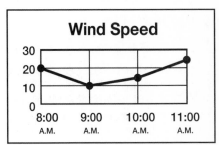

Wind Speed

30
20
10
0
8:00   9:00   10:00   11:00
A.M.   A.M.   A.M.   A.M.

Line Graph

Write the type of graph described. You will use one type of graph twice.

1. This type of graph shows parts of a whole. ___circle graph___

2. This type of graph uses a key instead of a scale. ___pictograph___

3. This type of graph shows change over time. ___line graph___

4. This type of graph compares amounts. ___bar graph___

5. This type of graph uses symbols instead of dots, bars, portions, or numbers. ___pictograph___

Copyright © Houghton Mifflin Company. All rights reserved.

Use with text pages 384–386.

Points, Lines, and Line Segments

Read the definitions.

segment	a part of something
endpoint	a point where a line stops
parallel	running beside a line, in exactly the same direction
perpendicular	crossing to form right angles
intersecting	having a meeting point

Follow the instructions.

1. This is a **line segment.** It has two **endpoints.**

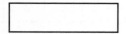

Draw another line segment in the the box below.

2. These lines are **parallel.**

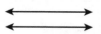

Draw another line that is parallel to the two lines above.

3. These lines are **perpendicular.**

Draw a line perpendicular to the line below.

4. These lines are **intersecting** lines.

Draw a line that intersects the line below.

5. Underline the correct answer.

(Parallel, <u>Perpendicular</u>) lines are intersecting lines.

1–4: Check that students have followed the directions properly and demonstrated understanding of lesson vocabulary.

Copyright © Houghton Mifflin Company. All rights reserved.

Use with text pages 404–406.

Rays and Angles

Study this information.

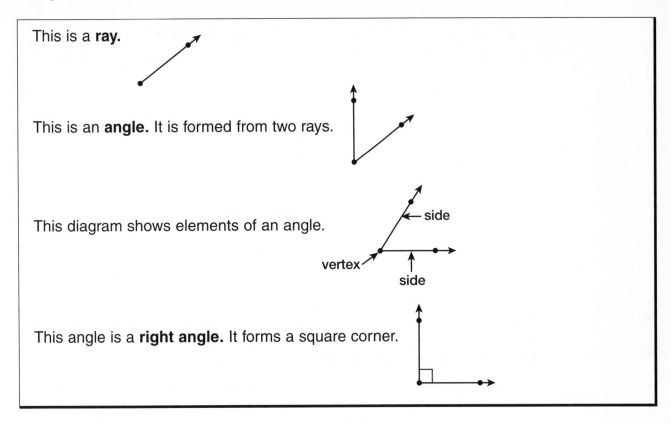

This is a **ray.**

This is an **angle.** It is formed from two rays.

This diagram shows elements of an angle.

side

vertex

side

This angle is a **right angle.** It forms a square corner.

Match each term with its definition.

1. **ray**   "formed by two rays with a common endpoint"

2. **angle**   "part of a line"

3. **vertex**   "an angle that makes a square corner"

4. **right angle**   "the common endpoint of the rays that make an angle"

5. **Draw lines from the labels to show the elements of this angle.**

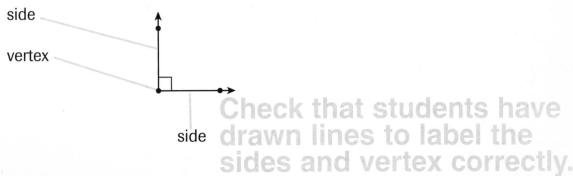

side

vertex

side

Check that students have drawn lines to label the sides and vertex correctly.

Copyright © Houghton Mifflin Company. All rights reserved.

Use with text pages 408–409.

Measure Angles

Study this information.

This angle is a **right angle**. It measures exactly 90°.	This angle is an **obtuse angle**. It is wider than a right angle.
This angle is an **acute angle**. It is not as wide as a right angle.	This angle is a **straight angle**. It measures exactly 180°.

Complete each sentence with a word from the box.

obtuse	straight	acute	right

1. The narrowest kind of angle is a(n) ____acute____ angle.

2. A(n) ____right____ angle is wider than an acute angle, but narrower than an obtuse angle.

3. A(n) ____obtuse____ angle is wider than a right angle, but narrower than a straight angle.

4. A(n) ____straight____ angle is the widest of these kinds of angles.

5. **Underline the correct answer.**

   An (acute, <u>obtuse</u>) angle is wider than a right angle.

Copyright © Houghton Mifflin Company. All rights reserved.

Quadrilaterals and Other Polygons

Read this information.

A **polygon** is a flat, closed plane figure. It has at least 3 sides. The sides are made of line segments.

A **regular polygon** has sides that are all equal in length.

An **irregular polygon** has sides that are not all equal in length.

A **rectangle** has four square corners. Its opposite sides are parallel.

A **trapezoid** has four sides. Only two are parallel.

Draw circles to answer these questions.

1. Which figure is a **polygon**?

2. Which figure is a **regular polygon**?

3. Which figure is an **irregular polygon**?

4. Which figure is a **rectangle**?

5. Which figure is a **trapezoid**?

 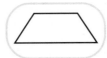

Copyright © Houghton Mifflin Company. All rights reserved.

Use with text pages 412–414.

Name _____ Date _____

Classify Triangles

Study this information.

An **equilateral** triangle has all sides of the same length.

An **isosceles** triangle has at least 2 sides that are the same length.

A **scalene** triangle has no sides that are the same length.

A **right** triangle has a right angle.

Draw circles to answer these questions.

1. Which figure is an equilateral triangle?

2. Which figure is an isosceles triangle?

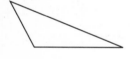 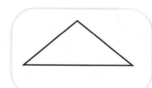

3. Which figure is a scalene triangle?

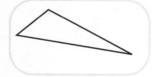

4. Which figure is a right triangle?

Copyright © Houghton Mifflin Company. All rights reserved.

Use with text pages 416–417.

Problem-Solving Strategy:
Find a Pattern

Study this information.

 The word part *tri* means "3." A triangle has 3 sides.

 The word part *quad* means "4." A quadrilateral has 4 sides.

 The word part *pent* means "5." A pentagon has 5 sides.

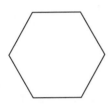 The word part *hex* means "6." A hexagon has 6 sides.

 The word part *oct* means "8." An octagon has 8 sides.

Complete each label by writing the correct word part from the box.

tri	quad	pent	hex	oct

1.

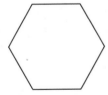

____hex____agon

2.

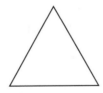

____tri____angle

3.

quadrilateral

4.

____oct____agon

5.

____pent____agon

Copyright © Houghton Mifflin Company. All rights reserved.

Use with text pages 418–420.

Circles

Look at the diagram.

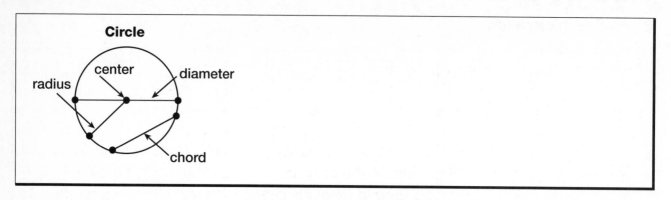

Match each term with its definition. Use the diagram to help you.

1. **circle**   any line segment that has its endpoints on a circle

2. **center**   a round figure; a figure made up of all points in a plane
                                       that are the same distance from one point

3. **radius**   a line segment that passes through the center of a circle
                                       and has its endpoints on the circle

4. **diameter**   any line segment that joins a point on a circle with the
                                       center of the circle

5. **chord**   the point in the middle of a circle

Circle *True* or *False*. Use the diagram above to help you.

6. The longest chord you can draw is the diameter.   (True)   False

7. The radius of a circle is always longer than the diameter.   True   (False)

Copyright © Houghton Mifflin Company. All rights reserved.

Use with text pages 422–424.

Name _____ Date _____

Congruent Figures

Read the explanation.

Two **congruent figures** have the same shape and the same size.
They can be in different positions and still be congruent.

Look at the figures on the right. Then answer the questions with *yes* or *no*.

1. Are the figures the same shape? __yes__

   Are the figures the same size? __no__

   Are the figures congruent? __no__

2. Are the figures the same shape? __no__

   Are the figures the same size? __yes*__

   Are the figures congruent? __no__

3. Are the figures the same shape? __yes__

   Are the figures the same size? __yes__

   Are the figures congruent? __yes__

4. Are the figures the same shape? __yes__

   Are the figures the same size? __yes__

   Are the figures congruent? __yes__

*Approximately.

Explain your answer.

5. Are the figures congruent? Why or why not?

   No, they are not congruent, because they are different sizes.

Copyright © Houghton Mifflin Company. All rights reserved.

Use with text pages 430–432.

Rotations, Reflections, and Translations

Read the comics. Then read the definitions.

In math, a **reflection** is a mirror image. The phrase **mirror image** means "the image you would see in a mirror."

To create a mirror image of a figure, you **flip** it over a line.

In math, a **rotation** turns a figure around a point. The phrase **around a point** means "moving around a spot."

To rotate a figure around a point, you **turn** it.

In math, a **translation** slides a figure from one place to another in a straight line.

To create a translation of a figure, you **slide** it in a straight line in any direction.

slide → slide

Circle the word that describes each transformation.

1. reflection   rotation   (translation)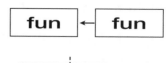

2. (reflection)   rotation   translation

3. reflection   (rotation)   translation

4. (reflection)   rotation   translation

5. reflection   (rotation)   translation

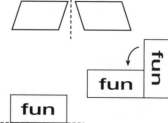

Copyright © Houghton Mifflin Company. All rights reserved.

Use with text pages 434–435.

Problem-Solving Strategy:
Act It Out

Look at these drawings. Read the explanations.

This snowflake **fits inside** the square. It does not overlap.

Each circle touches the next circle at **only one point.**

This snowflake is **overlapping** the square. It does not fit inside it.

Lesson Schedule	
4:00	Max
5:00	Beverly
6:00	Queenie
7:00	Marianne

On this **schedule,** the first lesson begins at 4:00.

Follow the instructions.

1. Draw a coin that fits inside this square.

Check that students' drawings fit entirely within the box.

2. Draw a coin that overlaps this square.

Check that students' drawings overlap the box.

3. Draw four circles in a row so that each circle touches the next circle at only one point.

Check that the circles students draw do not overlap; they should touch each other at one point.

4. Make a schedule. Make the first lesson begin at 1:00.

Lesson Schedule

Check students' schedules. Make sure that events are listed in time order.

Copyright © Houghton Mifflin Company. All rights reserved.

Use with text pages 436–438.

Name _____   Date _____

Symmetry

Read the paragraphs. Look at the drawings.

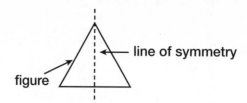

A figure can have **line symmetry.** That means that it can be folded along a line so that the two parts match exactly. The line created by the fold is called the **line of symmetry.** Plane figures that have symmetry can also be called **symmetrical.**

A figure can have more than one **line of symmetry.** The figure on the right has two lines of symmetry.

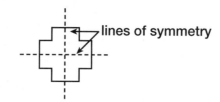

Draw circles to answer these questions.

1. Which figure has symmetry?

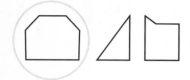

2. Which is a line of symmetry?

3. Which figure is symmetrical?

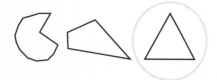

4. Which figure has 2 lines of symmetry shown?

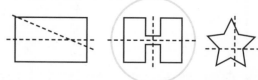

Copyright © Houghton Mifflin Company. All rights reserved.   **Use with text pages 440–443.**

Visual Thinking

Look at the drawings. Read the labels.

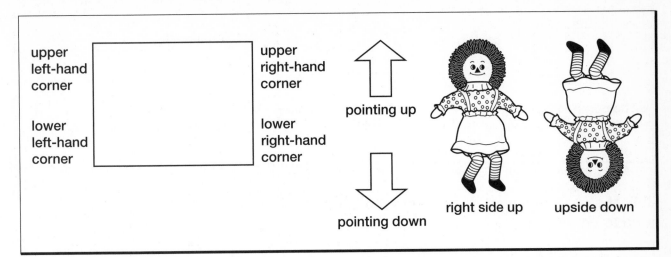

Follow the instructions.

1. Draw a star in the upper right-hand corner of this box.

1–5: Check that students have
followed the directions properly

2. Draw an X in the upper left-hand corner of this box.

and demonstrated understanding of lesson vocabulary.

3. Draw a line from the upper left-hand corner of this box
   to the lower right-hand corner.

4. Draw an arrow pointing up in the
   right-hand box. Draw an arrow
   pointing down in the left-hand box.

5. Draw a tree right side up in the
   left-hand box. Draw the same
   kind of tree upside down in the
   right-hand box.

Copyright © Houghton Mifflin Company. All rights reserved.

Use with text pages 444–446.

Name _____ Date _____

Explore Perimeter and Area

Read these explanations.

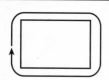   = 1 square unit

The **perimeter** of a figure
is the distance around it.

The **area** of a figure is the number of
square units needed to cover it.

**Tell whether you would need to find the perimeter or the
area to do each job.**

1. You work for a floor
   covering company.
   You must put squares
   of new linoleum on a
   kitchen floor.

____area____

2. You are a carpenter.
   You must build a
   fence all the way
   around a private
   garden.

____perimeter____

3. You sell cars. Your
   boss wants you to put
   up lights around the
   outside of the lot.

____perimeter____

4. You are a gardener.
   You must put in sod
   to make a new lawn
   for a family.

____area____

5. You plan to walk all
   the way around the
   state of Wyoming.

____perimeter____

Copyright © Houghton Mifflin Company. All rights reserved.

Use with text pages 452–453.

Perimeter

**Read the definitions. They tell how the
words are used in Lesson 2.**

diorama	a tiny scene with model figures
strip	a long, thin piece of something
leather	a material made from the hide of an animal
edging	something that forms the edge or border of an object or area
border	a decorative strip around the edge of something
sandals	shoes made of soles with straps
trace	to make an outline by drawing around the edge of something

Write words from the box to complete the sentences.

diorama	**strips**	**leather**	**edging**	**border**	**sandals**	**trace**

1. The Kimuras' new tablecloth has a fancy _____ .

2. Miss Fultz put plastic _____ around her lawn.

3. Kiki will _____ the outline of a mask and then cut out the shape.

4. On a hot day, it feels better to wear _____ than to wear boots.

5. Many shoes are made of _____ .

6. Lena made a _____ of an arctic beach using models of seals.

7. Roger cut _____ of meat to cook on the grill.

Copyright © Houghton Mifflin Company. All rights reserved.

Use with text pages 454–455.

Algebra: Area

Look at the pictures. Read the information.

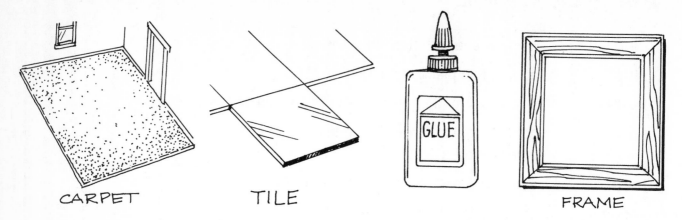

CARPET   TILE   GLUE   FRAME

Some words that can be used as nouns can also be used
as verbs.

noun: You can stick those pieces together with **glue.**

verb: Stephen will **glue** the plate back together.

noun: Yvonne likes the red **tile** better than the yellow tile.

verb: She will **tile** her kitchen this weekend.

noun: Orlo likes to walk on his new **carpet** with bare feet.

verb: Workers can **carpet** your stairs in just 4 hours.

noun: Wilson put a picture in the **frame.**

verb: Can you **frame** this photograph for me?

**Look for the word *glue, tile, frame,* or *carpet* in
each sentence. If it is used as a verb, underline
it. If it is used as a noun, circle it.**

1. Callie spilled glue on the rug.

2. That big blue tile is heavy.

3. You can tile the porch as soon as I finish painting the walls.

4. Lester will glue the pieces together for you.

5. The frame around the window is rotten.

6. Our company will carpet your playroom for only $1,000!

7. Mort will frame your painting if you ask him.

8. Do not spill salsa on the carpet.

Copyright © Houghton Mifflin Company. All rights reserved.

Use with text pages 456–458.

Algebra: Perimeter and Area of Complex Figures

Look at this table.

How Much Grass Seed to Buy	
Area (ft²)	Pounds of Seeds
1,000	1
1,500	2
2,000	3
2,500	4

Answer each question by writing a complete sentence. Answers will vary.

1. What does this table show?

It shows how many pounds of grass seed are needed to cover areas of different sizes with grass.

2. What is grass seed?

Grass seed is seed planted in order to grow a lawn.

3. What unit of measurement does *ft²* stand for?

It stands for square feet.

4. How much area will 1 pound of seed cover?

One pound of seed will cover 1,000 square feet.

5. What is the largest area shown on this chart?

The largest area shown is 2,500 square feet.

Copyright © Houghton Mifflin Company. All rights reserved.

Use with text pages 460–462.

Name _____ Date _____

Solid Figures and Nets

Look at these solid figures.

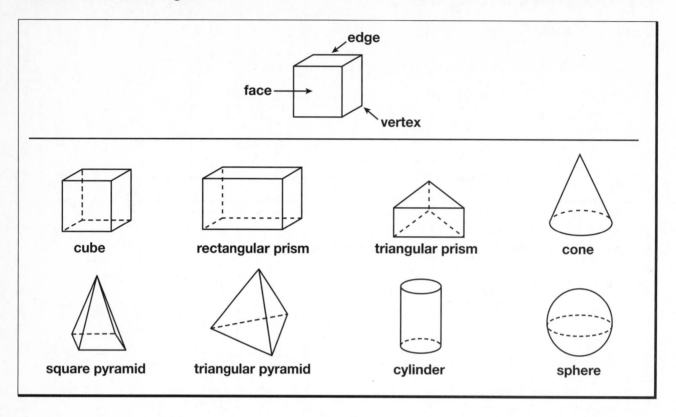

Read each clue. Write the name of the solid figure it describes.

1. I have one flat face. I come to a point. ___cone___

2. I have one square and four triangles. ___square pyramid___

3. I have no faces. ___sphere___

4. I have six squares. ___cube___

5. I have two flat faces. I can roll. ___cylinder___

6. I have four triangles but no rectangles. ___triangular pyramid___

7. I have two triangles and three rectangles. ___triangular prism___

8. I have six rectangles. ___rectangular prism___

Copyright © Houghton Mifflin Company. All rights reserved.

Use with text pages 464–467.

Algebra: Volume

Read this information.

The word endings *-arium* and *-orium* mean "a place for."

A *terrarium* is a small enclosure for growing plants.

An *aquarium* is a place for keeping and displaying fish and other sea creatures.

A *planetarium* is a place to see displays of planets and stars.

An *auditorium* is a place for large meetings and performances.

Write the name of each place or thing below its picture.

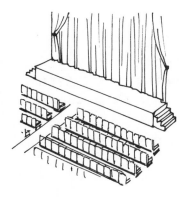

1. auditorium
_____

2. aquarium
_____

3. terrarium
_____

4. planetarium
_____

Copyright © Houghton Mifflin Company. All rights reserved.

Use with text pages 468–469.

Use Formulas

In English, a word can have many forms. Read these word forms and their parts of speech and definitions.

decorate (verb)	to adorn with beautiful things
decoration (noun)	an object used to make something look pretty or fancy
decorator (noun)	a person whose job it is to choose nice-looking furniture and decorations
decorative (adjective)	serving to make prettier
decor (noun)	the furniture and decorations in a home or building

Use a word form from the box to complete each sentence.

| decorate | decoration | decorator | decorative | decor |

1. The owners of the mansion hired a _____ to make the downstairs rooms look nicer.

2. The person they hired will _____ the hall with new rugs and paintings.

3. "This old doll will make a nice _____ in the living room," she said.

4. The sofa she has chosen has _____ lace on its arms.

5. The new _____ will make the big house seem friendlier.

Copyright © Houghton Mifflin Company. All rights reserved.

Use with text pages 470–472.

Represent Fractions

Look at these diagrams of fractions. Read the words that name the portions.

($\frac{1}{2}$ $\frac{1}{2}$)	divided into **halves**	(sevenths circle)	divided into **sevenths**
(thirds circle)	divided into **thirds**	(eighths circle)	divided into **eighths**
(fourths circle)	divided into **fourths, or quarters**	(ninths circle)	divided into **ninths**
(fifths circle)	divided into **fifths**	(tenths circle)	divided into **tenths**
(sixths circle)	divided into **sixths**		

Use the words in bold type to answer these questions.

1. If a pie is cut into 8 equal pieces, it is divided into _____eighths_____.

2. If a pizza is cut into 6 equal pieces, it is divided into _____sixths_____.

3. If a pancake is cut into 2 equal pieces, the pieces are called _____halves_____.

4. If a cake is cut into 7 equal pieces, it is divided into _____sevenths_____.

5. If a round loaf of bread is cut into 5 equal pieces, it is divided into _____fifths_____.

6. If a tortilla from Spain is cut into 9 equal pieces, it is divided into _____ninths_____.

7. If a wheel of cheese is cut into 10 equal wedges, it is divided into _____tenths_____.

8. If a piece of pita bread is cut into 4 equal pieces, it is divided

   into _____fourths_____, or _____quarters_____.

Copyright © Houghton Mifflin Company. All rights reserved.

Use with text pages 490–491.

Explore Equivalent Fractions

Read these definitions of related word forms.

equal	having the same value, measure, or quantity
equivalent	naming the same amount
equitable	fair, impartial
equation	a mathematical sentence stating that two quantities are equal
equity	the quality of being fair and impartial
equality	the quality of being equal

Draw a line under the correct word in each sentence.

1. $\dfrac{x}{4} = \dfrac{2}{8}$

Luther needed to solve a math problem, so he wrote an (equity, <u>equation</u>).

2. When all people in a nation are treated equal, its people have achieved (<u>equality</u>, equation).

3. $\dfrac{1}{3} = \dfrac{2}{6}$

The fractions $\dfrac{1}{3}$ and $\dfrac{2}{6}$ are called (equity, <u>equivalent</u>) fractions because they name the same amount.

4. 17, 8, 55

When added together, the numbers above (equitable, <u>equal</u>) 80.

5. The judge was respected by the citizens because of the (equivalent, <u>equity</u>) of his decisions.

6. The principal's decision was (equal, <u>equitable</u>), so everyone felt good about it.

Copyright © Houghton Mifflin Company. All rights reserved.

Use with text pages 492–493.

Equivalent Fractions and Simplest Form

Read these definitions.

shake	a thick drink made in a fast mixing machine
cranberry	a small, round, sour red berry
pineapple	a large, sweet yellow fruit with a rough outside covering
banana	a long white fruit with yellow or green skin
juice	liquid squeezed from a fruit
serving	an amount for one person to eat or drink

Use words from the box to make the sentences tell about the drawings.

shake	cranberry	pineapple	bananas	juice	serving

Denise made a face when she bit into the little red _____ cranberry _____.

Mrs. Macias squeezes oranges to make _____ juice _____.

You must cut a _____ pineapple _____ carefully to get to the sweet fruit.

Miss Ting ordered one _____ serving _____ of fruit salad.

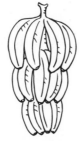

Some kinds of _____ bananas _____ are ripe when they are green.

A fruit _____ shake _____ has fruit in it, and something to make it thick.

Copyright © Houghton Mifflin Company. All rights reserved.

Use with text pages 494–496.

Compare and Order Fractions

Study this chart.

Use to Describe	Use to Compare 2 Things	Use to Compare More Than 2 Things
easy	easier	easiest
little	less	least
great	greater	greatest
long	longer	longest

Underline the correct form in each sentence.

1. It is (easier, easiest) to peel a banana than it is to peel a pumpkin.

2. Paula says that bananas are the (easier, easiest) fruit to peel.

3. $\frac{1}{5}$ of a pie is (less, least) than $\frac{1}{3}$ of a pie.

4. Among the fractions $\frac{1}{5}$, $\frac{3}{10}$, and $\frac{4}{5}$, $\frac{1}{5}$ is the (less, least).

5. $\frac{1}{2}$ cup is a (greater, greatest) amount than $\frac{3}{8}$ cup.

6. Among the fractions $\frac{1}{4}$, $\frac{7}{8}$, and $\frac{5}{8}$, $\frac{7}{8}$ is the (greater, greatest).

7. October is a (longer, longest) month than September.

8. Beth's hose is 10 feet long. Bill's hose is 15 feet long. Irv's hose is 18 feet long. Pat's hose is 20 feet long. Pat's hose is the (longer, longest) hose of all.

Copyright © Houghton Mifflin Company. All rights reserved.

Use with text pages 498–500.

Find Part of a Number

Read this information.

Sometimes you need to find the number of items represented by a fraction.

Vichhana has 12 buttons. Two thirds of the buttons are silver. How many silver buttons does she have?

You can solve this problem by dividing and then multiplying.

STEP 1:

number of   number of
buttons   equal groups

$$12 \div 3 = 4$$

number of buttons in each group

STEP 2:

number of groups   number of
of silver buttons   silver buttons

$$4 \times 2 = 8$$

number of buttons in each group

Read the problem. Label each part of the solution with a phrase from the box.

Rex has 10 posters. Three fifths of them show whales. How many whale posters does he have?

number of equal groups	number of whale posters
number of posters in each group	number of posters

STEP 1:

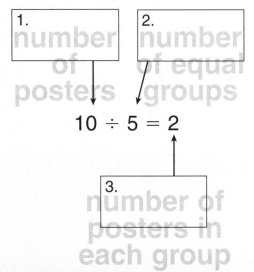

1. number
of
posters

2. number
of equal
groups

$$10 \div 5 = 2$$

3. number of
posters in
each group

STEP 2:

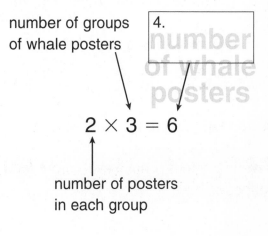

number of groups
of whale posters

4. number
of whale
posters

$$2 \times 3 = 6$$

number of posters
in each group

Copyright © Houghton Mifflin Company. All rights reserved.

Use with text pages 502–503.

Problem-Solving Strategy: Draw a Picture

Look at this picture dictionary.

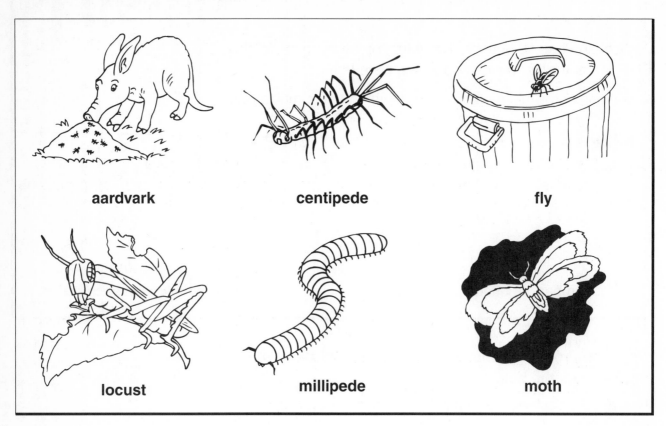

aardvark	centipede	fly
locust	millipede	moth

Use the picture dictionary to help you solve these riddles. Write the answers on the lines.

1. I have big wings. I fly toward lights. _____ moth

2. I am a large insect. I eat crops. _____ locust

3. I am small and black. I love garbage. _____ fly

4. I have many legs, but not as many as a millipede. _____ centipede

5. I have a long snout. I love to eat ants. _____ aardvark

6. I have many legs. I have even more legs than centipedes have. _____ millipede

Copyright © Houghton Mifflin Company. All rights reserved.

Use with text pages 504–506.

Mixed Numbers and Improper Fractions

Read this information.

> The prefix *in-* or *im-* can mean "not." When you add *in-* or *im-*
> to a word, you often create a word with the opposite meaning.
>
> **Complete** means "having all the parts needed."
>
> **Incomplete** means "not having all the parts needed."
>
> **Proper** means "appropriate."
>
> **Improper** means "not appropriate."
>
> In math, a **proper fraction** has a numerator that is **less than**
> its denominator. An **improper fraction** has a numerator that is
> **equal to or more than** its denominator.

Underline the word that makes sense in each sentence.

1. Woodrow is a rude person. He is (polite, <u>impolite</u>) to
   almost everyone.

2. Venetta wanted to get to school quickly, so she chose the
   most (<u>direct</u>, indirect) route.

3. Corazon wrote $\frac{6}{5}$ and $\frac{9}{4}$ on the board. These are
   (proper, <u>improper</u>) fractions.

4. Tali wrote $\frac{5}{6}$ and $\frac{4}{9}$ on the board. These are
   (<u>proper</u>, improper) fractions.

5. Jamar has finished his report. It is (<u>complete</u>, incomplete).

Copyright © Houghton Mifflin Company. All rights reserved.

Use with text pages 508–510.

Add and Subtract Fractions
With Like Denominators

Read these rules.

Some verbs add *-ed* to talk about the past.

    We **row** often.   ⟶   We **rowed** fast
                                    yesterday.

Some verbs change form to talk about the past.

    We **swim** often.   ⟶   We **swam** fast
                                      yesterday.

Verbs can add *-ing* and be used with *is, are, was,*
or *were.*

    We **are rowing** fast.

rowing

swimming

Draw a line under the correct verb.

1. This morning Daisy (<u>rowed</u>, rowing) a boat by herself.

2. Howard is (rowed, <u>rowing</u>) a new boat now.

3. A big fish is (swam, <u>swimming</u>) near the boat.

4. Howard and Daisy (swimmed, <u>swam</u>) in a pool last Friday.

Complete each sentence. Write *rowed* or *rowing*.

5. Yesterday Daisy and Howard _____*rowed*_____ across the lake.

6. They were _____*rowing*_____ fast all the way across.

Complete each sentence. Write *swam* or *swimming*.

7. Last Tuesday Daisy _____*swam*_____ in a pool.

8. She was _____*swimming*_____ for two hours.

Copyright © Houghton Mifflin Company. All rights reserved.

Use with text pages 516–519.

Add and Subtract Mixed Numbers

Study these steps for adding mixed numbers.

Add.

$2\frac{1}{4} + 1\frac{1}{4} = \square$

STEP 1: Add the fractions.	**STEP 2:** Add the whole numbers.	Write the answer in simplest form.
$2\frac{1}{4}$ $+\ 1\frac{1}{4}$ $\overline{\quad\frac{2}{4}}$	$2\frac{1}{4}$ $+\ 1\frac{1}{4}$ $\overline{3\frac{2}{4}}$	$= 3\frac{1}{2}$

Study these steps for subtracting mixed numbers. Then use words from the box to fill in the blanks.

simplest	subtract	fractions

Subtract.

$1\frac{3}{8} - \frac{1}{8} = \square$

STEP 1: Subtract the 1. ___fractions___.	**STEP 2:** 2. ___Subtract___ the whole numbers.	Write the answer in 3. ___simplest___ form.
$1\frac{3}{8}$ $-\ \frac{1}{8}$ $\overline{\quad\frac{2}{8}}$	$1\frac{3}{8}$ $-\ \frac{1}{8}$ $\overline{1\frac{2}{8}}$	$= 1\frac{1}{4}$

Underline the correct word in each sentence.

4. When you add mixed numbers, you add the (<u>fractions</u>, whole numbers) first.

5. When you subtract mixed numbers, you subtract the (<u>fractions</u>, whole numbers) first.

Copyright © Houghton Mifflin Company. All rights reserved.

Use with text pages 520–521.

Problem-Solving Application: Decide How to Write the Quotient

Read the explanations.

A **safari park** is a park where visitors can see wild animals from Africa on open land.

A **parent** is an adult who has one or more children.

A **jungle tram** is a small train that takes visitors around a safari park or other area with wild animals.

An **animal keeper** is a person who helps care for animals in a safari park or zoo.

A **rhinoceros** is a very large mammal with a horn on its nose.

Alfalfa is a grass that is good food for many animals.

A **zoo shop** is a place where books about animals are sold.

A **camel ride** is a ride on the back of a camel.

Label each picture with a term from the box.

safari park	parent	jungle tram	animal keeper
rhinoceros	alfalfa	zoo shop	camel ride

1. camel ride   2. parent   3. zoo shop   4. rhinoceros

5. animal keeper   6. jungle tram   7. safari park   8. alfalfa

Copyright © Houghton Mifflin Company. All rights reserved.

Use with text pages 522–523.

Estimate With Fractions

Read these definitions.

hike	to take a long walk
trail	a path through a wild area or a park
falls	water from a creek or river falling down a cliff or hillside
mine	a tunnel dug to get minerals out of the earth
hiker	a person who takes long walks in wild areas

Use words from the box to complete the sentences.

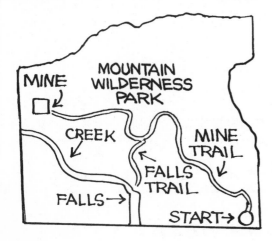

hike	trail	falls	mine	hiker

1. Zoila has taken many long walks through the mountains. She is an experienced

   _____hiker_____.

2. She wants to _____hike_____ all day in the park.

3. First she wants to go to the _____mine_____. It is a place where workers
   once dug gold out of the earth.

4. Then she wants to go to the _____falls_____. It is a place where water goes
   over the edge of a cliff.

5. She will always stay on the _____trail_____ when she walks. She knows it is
   not a good idea to walk where there are no paths.

Copyright © Houghton Mifflin Company. All rights reserved.

Use with text pages 524–525.

Name _____   Date _____

Problem-Solving Decision: Choose a Method

Read these problems. Pay attention to the words in bold type. These key words help you know what to do to solve the problem.

Problem	What to Do
Ingrid rode her bike $2\frac{1}{2}$ miles, $1\frac{1}{4}$ miles, and $3\frac{1}{8}$ miles in three days. **How many** miles did she ride in three days?	add
Nate rode his bike $\frac{9}{10}$ mile before noon and $\frac{3}{10}$ mile after. **How much farther** did he ride before noon than after?	subtract
Stanlee rode his bike 21 miles in 3 days. **How many** miles did he **average** per day?	divide
Beth has 3 packages of bike safety books. There are 3 books **in each** package. How many books does she have **in all**?	multiply

Underlined words may vary.

Read each problem. Underline the key words. Write what you would do to solve the problem.

1. Montel fixed 8 bikes in 4 days. How many bikes did he average fixing per day?

   divide

2. Sandy rode $\frac{3}{4}$ mile in the morning and $\frac{1}{4}$ mile in the afternoon. How much farther did she ride in the morning?

   subtract

3. Ollie has 3 sheets of bike stamps. There are 6 stamps on each sheet. How many stamps does he have in all?

   multiply

4. Belinda rode $1\frac{1}{2}$ miles Monday, $2\frac{1}{2}$ miles Tuesday, and $3\frac{1}{2}$ miles Wednesday. How many miles did she ride in 3 days?

   add

Copyright © Houghton Mifflin Company. All rights reserved.

Use with text page 526.

Name _____ Date _____

Add Fractions With Unlike Denominators

Read the information.

The prefix **un-** means "not" or "the opposite of."

like	"the same or similar"
unlike	"not the same; different"

Circle the word that makes the phrase fit the drawing.

(friendly, unfriendly)
dogs

(happy, unhappy)
children

(tidy, untidy)
desks

$\frac{3}{4} + \frac{7}{8}$

(like, unlike)
denominators

(tidy, untidy)
tables

$\frac{5}{6} + \frac{1}{6}$

(like, unlike)
denominators

(safe, unsafe)
stairs

(tied, untied)
shoes

(safe, unsafe)
riders

Copyright © Houghton Mifflin Company. All rights reserved.

Use with text pages 528–529.

Subtract Fractions With Unlike Denominators

Read these explanations of expressions used in the lesson.

> **The remaining space** means "the space not covered up."
>
> **Like fraction pieces** means "pieces for fractions that have the same numerator and denominator."
>
> **Line up** means "place end-to-end."
>
> The **difference** is the name for the answer to a subtraction problem.

Look at each item below. Find the expression in the box that tells what it shows. Write the expression on the line.

remaining space	like fraction pieces	line up	difference

1. _____ line up _____

2. _____ remaining space _____

$$\frac{1}{2} - \frac{1}{3} = \frac{1}{6}$$

3. _____ difference _____

4. _____ like fraction pieces _____

Copyright © Houghton Mifflin Company. All rights reserved.

Use with text pages 530–532.

Name _____ Date _____

Problem-Solving Application:
Use a Circle Graph

Look at the pictures. Read the sentences. Pay attention to the words in bold type.

beads

Olivia used **beads** to make a big **bracelet**.

bracelet

She did not make the **bracelet** to wear on her wrist.

She made the bracelet as a **collar** for her dog.

First Mark tried **woodworking.** He worked to shape and smooth a piece of wood.

Next, Mark tried **weaving.** He used a loom to make yarn into cloth.

Then Mark tried **pottery.** He used a potter's wheel to make a round pot.

Draw lines to match the terms to their definitions.

1. beads   something that goes around the neck

2. bracelet   making objects out of clay

3. collar   small objects with holes drilled through them

4. woodworking   a round object that is worn around the wrist

5. weaving   making objects by shaping and joining pieces of wood

6. pottery   making cloth from yarn

Copyright © Houghton Mifflin Company. All rights reserved.

Use with text pages 534–536.

Name _____ Date _____

Tenths and Hundredths

Read this information.

When a fraction has a denominator of 10, it tells about a whole with ten parts. These parts are called **tenths.** You use this word to talk and write about the values of fractions with the denominator 10.

$\frac{1}{10}$ = 1 **tenth** $\frac{7}{10}$ = 7 **tenths**

When a fraction has a denominator of 100, it tells about a whole with one hundred parts. These parts are called **hundredths.** You use this word to talk and write about the values of fractions with the denominator 100.

$\frac{1}{100}$ = 1 **hundredth** $\frac{25}{100}$ = 25 **hundredths**

Write the value of each fraction. Use a number for the numerator. Use a word for the denominator.

1. $\frac{4}{10}$ _____4 tenths_____

2. $\frac{28}{100}$ _____28 hundredths_____

3. $\frac{2}{10}$ _____2 tenths_____

4. $\frac{99}{100}$ _____99 hundredths_____

5. $\frac{1}{10}$ _____1 tenth_____

6. $\frac{7}{100}$ _____7 hundredths_____

7. $\frac{5}{10}$ _____5 tenths_____

8. $\frac{1}{100}$ _____1 hundredth_____

9. $\frac{30}{100}$ _____30 hundredths_____

10. $\frac{8}{10}$ _____8 tenths_____

Circle the correct term.

11. 2 tens   (2 tenths)

12. (2 tens)   2 tenths

Copyright © Houghton Mifflin Company. All rights reserved.

Use with text pages 542–543.

Thousandths

Read this information.

When you write a number between 21 and 99 that is made up of two words, use a **hyphen** (-).

21 = **twenty-one**   63 = **sixty-three**

Do this even if the number is part of a larger number.

184 = one hundred **eighty-four**
2,626 = two thousand six hundred **twenty-six**

Do this also when writing a fraction in words.

$\frac{28}{100}$ = **twenty-eight** hundredths
$\frac{149}{1,000}$ = one hundred **forty-nine** thousandths

Write each number in words. Use hyphens where they are needed.

1. 35 _thirty-five_

2. 77 _seventy-seven_

3. 84 _eighty-four_

4. 56 _fifty-six_

5. 129 _one hundred twenty-nine_

6. 558 _five hundred fifty-eight_

7. 1,794 _one thousand seven hundred ninety-four_

8. 3,262 _three thousand two hundred sixty-two_

Write each fraction in words. Use hyphens where they are needed.

9. $\frac{52}{100}$ _fifty-two hundredths_

10. $\frac{685}{1,000}$ _six hundred eighty-five thousandths_

Copyright © Houghton Mifflin Company. All rights reserved.

Use with text pages 544–545.

Mixed Numbers and Decimals

Look at these different ways to show one and five tenths.

Models	Mixed Number	Place Value Chart
	$1\frac{5}{10}$	**ones** . **tenths** / 1 . 5
Standard Form	**Word Form**	**Expanded Form**
1.5	one and five tenths	$1 + 0.5$

Choose the label from the box that tells how the fraction $2\frac{1}{10}$ is shown in each item below. Write the label on the line.

models	mixed number	place value chart
standard form	word form	expanded form

1.

ones		tenths
2	.	1

place value chart

2. two and one tenth

word form

3.

models

4. 2.1

standard form

5. $2 + 0.1$

expanded form

6. $2\frac{1}{10}$

mixed number

Copyright © Houghton Mifflin Company. All rights reserved.

Use with text pages 546–548.

Fractions and Decimal Equivalents

**It is important to read math problems carefully.
One word can make a big difference!**

**Read this problem and the answer a student gave.
Circle the word that the student did not read.**

Write a decimal that tells the part of the balloons that is not dark. __0.4__

If you circled **not**, you are correct. The part of the balloons that is **not** dark is 0.6, not 0.4.

**Read each problem. Circle the most important words to notice.
You do not have to solve the problems.**

1. Write a number that tells how many hats are dark.

2. Write a decimal that tells the part of the hats that are light.

3. Write a number that tells how many hats are not light.

4. Write a decimal that tells the part of the hats that are not dark.

5. Write a decimal that tells the part of the hats that are not light.

6. Write a number that tells how many hats are not dark.

1–6: Students should circle words that are important to solving the problems, such as *how many, the part of, number, decimal, dark, light,* and *not.*

Copyright © Houghton Mifflin Company. All rights reserved.

Use with text pages 550–552.

Find a Pattern

**Read this paragraph. Think about the meanings
of the words in bold type.**

Oleg is a member of an **ice-skating club.**
He and the other club members practice ice-
skating as a group several times a week. Last
week a photographer came to take pictures of
skating highlights. She took photos of Oleg's
best jumps and spins. Next week she will offer
photo packages to the club members. Each
skater's package will have 5 small photos of his
or her best jumps and spins. It will also have
one **skating photo enlargement** in it. This will
be a large-sized copy of the best photo. Oleg is
not sure whether he will buy his photo package.
He needs money to buy some pairs of **skate
laces.** If he does not have good laces, he
cannot tie his skates.

Use the phrases in the box to answer these questions.

| ice-skating club | skating highlights | photo package |
| skating photo enlargement | | skate laces |

1. You use these to keep ice skates on your feet. _____ skate laces

2. You join this if you want to skate with other people. _____ ice-skating club

3. You buy this if you want several photos of yourself. _____ photo package

4. These are the best jumps, spins, and other moves
   you perform on the ice. _____ skating highlights

5. This is a large copy of an ice-skating photo. _____ skating photo
   enlargement

Copyright © Houghton Mifflin Company. All rights reserved.

Use with text pages 554–556.

Compare and Order Decimals

Read this information.

In English, many words can be used as a noun or as a verb.

meet   *noun*   a competition involving races and other events

meet   *verb*   to have contact with a person for the first time or to get together with someone at a particular time and place

score   *noun*   the number of points a person or team has

score   *verb*   to earn one or more points by doing something

Write *meet, meets, score,* or *scores* to complete each sentence. Circle each word you write that is used as a verb.

1. Olajane and Marlette will compete in the swim _____ meet _____ this Saturday.

2. Olajane will _____ (meet) _____ Marlette at the bus stop, and the two of them will take the bus together.

3. Olajane usually _____ (scores) _____ points for her team in short swim races.

4. Marlette will probably earn a high _____ score _____ in the diving competition.

5. After the _____ meet _____ is over, Marlette will _____ (meet) _____ her father at the store where he works.

6. She always tells him the _____ score _____ of the meet.
   or scores

Copyright © Houghton Mifflin Company. All rights reserved.

Use with text pages 558–559.

Compare and Order Decimals and Mixed Numbers

Look at the number lines. Read the information.

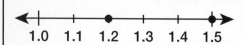
1.0 1.1 1.2 1.3 1.4 1.5

The decimal 1.2 is to the left of the decimal 1.5 on the number line.

1.2 < 1.5.

1.0 1.1 1.2 1.3 1.4 1.5

The decimal 1.5 is to the right of the decimal 1.2 on the number line.

1.5 > 1.2.

The phrase to **the left of** and the symbol < are used to compare two numbers. They help you to know that the decimal 1.2 is **less than** the decimal 1.5.

The phrase to **the right of** and the symbol > are used to compare two numbers. They help you to know that the decimal 1.5 is **greater than** the decimal 1.2.

Compare the numbers. Write *less than* or *greater than* in each blank.

1. 4.9 is ___greater than___ 3.9.

2. 1.0 is ___less than___ 11.1.

Use the number line to compare the numbers. Write *to the left of* or *to the right of* in each blank.

1.0 1.1 1.2 1.3 1.4 1.5 1.6 1.7

3. 1.6 is ___to the left of___ 1.7.   **4.** 1.5 is ___to the right of___ 1.2.

Compare the numbers. Write < or > in each blank.

5. 2.1 ___>___ 1.2.

6. 7.7 ___<___ 7.8.

Copyright © Houghton Mifflin Company. All rights reserved.

Use with text pages 560–562.

Name _____ Date _____

Round Decimals

Read these explanations.

Ghana is a nation in West Africa. It has a population of 12 million.

An **outdoor market** is an outside area where people sell fruits, vegetables, clothing, and other things.

Kola nuts are nuts from kola trees. They are used to make soft drinks and medicines.

Yams are vegetables. The yam plant has green vines that grow above the ground, and thick roots that grow below the ground.

Use a term from the box to label each picture.

Ghana	outdoor market	kola nuts	yam

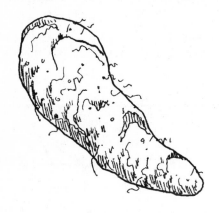

yam

1. _____

outdoor market

2. _____

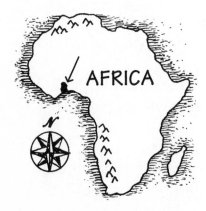

Ghana

3. _____

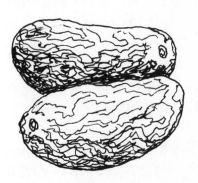

kola nuts

4. _____

Copyright © Houghton Mifflin Company. All rights reserved.

Use with text pages 568–569.

Estimate Decimal Sums and Differences

Read this information and the examples.

In English, you place **more** in front of long adjectives to compare two things.

reasonable → **more** reasonable

Example:

The students in a math class tried to guess how many dried peas it would take to fill a jar. Cyd's estimate was **more reasonable** than Paloma's estimate.

You place **most** in front of long adjectives to compare more than two things.

reasonable → **most** reasonable

Example:

In all, twenty-seven students estimated how many dried peas it would take to fill the jar. Val's estimate was the **most reasonable** of all.

Draw a line under the correct term.

1. Kurt and Roz tried to figure out how much fabric to buy to make a kite. Kurt's estimate was (more reasonable, most reasonable) than Roz's estimate.

2. Kurt, Roz, and William each estimated how much string they would need for the kite they were making. William's estimate was the (reasonablest, most reasonable).

3. Roz estimated that they would need 2 meters of bamboo to make the kite. William thought they would need 6 meters. Roz's estimate was (reasonabler, more reasonable).

4. Kurt, Roz, and William each estimated how much time it would take to make the kite. William's estimate was the (more reasonable, most reasonable).

Copyright © Houghton Mifflin Company. All rights reserved.

Use with text pages 570–571.

Explore Addition and Subtraction of Decimals

Some expressions used in math are made up of a verb and an adverb. Read these expressions and their meanings.

line up	align or put items in a horizontal or vertical line
cross out	draw an *X* through
take away	remove or subtract
look back	look again

Use an expression from the box to fill each blank.

line up	**cross out**	**take away**	**look back**

1. To check an answer, you should _____ at the problem, read it again, and look at your answer a second time.

2. To show that something on a list has been taken away, you can _____ that thing.

3. To add numbers, you must _____ the numbers correctly.

4. To subtract 7.1 from 88.3, you must first _____ the 1 in the tenths column from the 3 in that column.

Write answers to these questions.

5. To review something, do you **look back** or **look out**? _____

6. To remove something, do you **take it away** or **take it over**?
_____

7. To put things in a column, do you **line them down** or **line them up**?
_____

8. To show that an item on a list has been used, would you **cross out** or **cross over** that item? _____

Copyright © Houghton Mifflin Company. All rights reserved.

Use with text pages 572–573.

Add and Subtract Decimals

Read this explanation.

The word **total** often tells you that you must **add** to solve a problem.

Example: One car is 4.3 meters long. The other car is 5.1 meters long. What is the **total** length of the two cars?   ⟶   You must **add** 4.3 and 5.1 to solve this problem.

The word **remaining** often tells you that you must **subtract** to solve a problem.

Example: The height of three flights of stairs is 14.7 meters. Two flights have a height of 10.1 meters. What is the height of the **remaining** flight of stairs?   ⟶   You must **subtract** 10.1 from 14.7 to solve this problem.

In each problem below, circle the word *total* or the word *remaining*. Then write whether you would *add* or *subtract* to solve the problem.

1. The length of four benches is 8.8 meters. The length of two of the benches is 4.2 meters. What is the length of the (remaining) benches? __subtract__

2. The heights of three sets of shelves are 1.7 meters, 1.5 meters, and 1.2 meters. What would be the (total) height of the shelves if they were stacked on top of one another? __add__

3. Dalvin's table is 3.5 meters long. Lily's table is 4.4 meters long. What would be the (total) length of the tables if they were placed end to end? __add__

4. The height of five crates stacked on top of each other is 5.7 meters. The bottom three crates are 3.6 meters high. Find the height of the two (remaining) crates if they were stacked separately. __subtract__

Copyright © Houghton Mifflin Company. All rights reserved.

Use with text pages 574–575.

Name _____   Date _____

Name _____   Date _____

Problem-Solving Application: Use Decimals

Read these definitions.

subway system	a system of trains that run through underground tunnels
Tube line	a route in the London subway system
Tube station	a place in the London subway system where passengers get on and off
deep level	far under the ground
rail tunnel	a hole dug for a train or subway to travel through
one-day pass	a ticket that allows a person to ride a subway an unlimited amount of times in one day

Solve each riddle by writing an expression from the box.

subway system	**Tube line**	**Tube station**
deep level	**rail tunnel**	**one-day pass**

1. If you buy this today, it will let you ride a subway until midnight.

   one-day pass

2. This is dug so a subway train can travel through it. _rail tunnel_

3. This is made up of many lines and can take passengers all over a city.

   subway system

4. This means "at a level that is very deep in the ground." _deep level_

5. This is where you would go to get on a train in the London subway system.

   Tube station

6. This is one route in the London subway system. _Tube line_

Copyright © Houghton Mifflin Company. All rights reserved. **Use with text pages 576–578.**

Name _____ Date _____

Probability

Read the explanations.

An **event** is something that happens.

If an event is **certain,** that means that it will always happen.

If an event is **likely,** that means that it will happen most of the time.

If an event is **unlikely,** that means that it will not happen very often.

If an event is **impossible,** that means that it will never happen.

Look at the pictures and read the sentences. Write a word from the box that goes with each picture.

certain	impossible	likely	unlikely

The boy with the baseball cap will get a drink of water.

1. _____ likely

After the sun sets, the sky will become darker.

2. _____ certain

The ball will climb up the steps by itself.

3. _____ impossible

A coin will come up "heads" ten times in a row.

4. _____ unlikely

The tadpole will grow into a frog.

5. _____ certain (or likely)

The page after page 6 will be page 7.

6. _____ certain (or likely)

Copyright © Houghton Mifflin Company. All rights reserved.

Use with text pages 596–597.

Name _____   Date _____

Probability as a Fraction

Read this information.

Words that have the same or almost the same meaning are
called **synonyms.**

Study these synonyms.

likely—probable	**outcome—result**
favorable—positive	**pick—choose**
desired—wanted	**spin—rotate**

**Rewrite each sentence. Replace the word in
bold type with a synonym from the box.**

result	select	positive
probable	rotate	wanted

1. Jean and Toni are playing a game in which
   they **spin** a spinner and move markers on a board.

   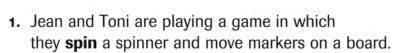

   Jean and Toni are playing a game in which they
   rotate a spinner and move markers on a board.

2. Jean thought it was **likely** that she would land on a safe square.

   Jean thought it was probable that she would
   land on a safe square.

3. If she landed on the blue square, she would have to **pick** a card from the pile.

   If she landed on the blue square, she would
   have to select a card from the pile.

4. The best **outcome** would be to land on the square that said "Take a free turn."

   The best result would be to land on the square
   that said "Take a free turn."

5. The number that the spin landed on was not the number Jean **desired.**

   The number that the spin landed on was not
   the number Jean wanted.

6. The outcome of that spin was unfavorable for Jean, but quite **favorable** for Toni.

   The outcome of that spin was unfavorable for
   Jean, but quite positive for Toni.

Copyright © Houghton Mifflin Company. All rights reserved.

Use with text pages 598–600.

Name _____   Date _____

Make Predictions

Read the definitions.

predict	to say what is likely to happen
put back	to return something to its place
land on	to end up in a place after moving
label	to mark something so it can be identified
record	to write down
compare	to see how two or more things are the same or different

Write words from the box to complete these sentences.

label	put back	lands on	predict	record	compare

1. In this experiment, Nils and Kevin must _____ *predict* _____ what card is likely to be picked.

2. Kevin will _____ *record* _____ the result on the tally chart.

3. Nils must _____ *put back* _____ the card he has picked before he draws another one.

4. After they finish the experiment, the boys will _____ *compare* _____ their results with those of other students.

5. For the next experiment, Nils and Kevin must _____ *label* _____ a cube with 6 letters.

6. Then they must roll the cube and record the letter it _____ *lands on* _____.

Copyright © Houghton Mifflin Company. All rights reserved.

Use with text pages 602–603.

Name _____ Date _____

Problem-Solving Strategy:
Make an Organized List

Look at the picture dictionary.

cello	daffodil	drum	flute
hyacinth	landscape	lily	portrait
saxophone	still life	tulip	violin

List each item from the picture dictionary in the correct category.

musical instruments

1. _cello_
2. _saxophone_
3. _drum_
4. _flute_
5. _violin_
Items 1–5 may be listed in any order.

flowers

6. _hyacinth_
7. _daffodil_
8. _lily_
9. _tulip_
Items 6–9 may be listed in any order.

types of paintings

10. _landscape_
11. _still life_
12. _portrait_
Items 10–12 may be listed in any order.

Copyright © Houghton Mifflin Company. All rights reserved.

Use with text pages 604–606.

Name _____ Date _____

Find Probability

**Look at the grid. Read the sentences that explain
what it shows.**

		Second Toss	
		heads	tails
First	heads	heads, heads	heads, tails
Toss	tails	tails, heads	tails, tails

If you toss heads first and heads second, the outcome is
heads, heads.

If you toss heads first and tails second, the outcome is **heads, tails.**

If you toss tails first and heads second, the outcome is **tails, heads.**

If you toss tails first and tails second, the outcome is **tails, tails.**

**Look at this grid. Fill in the blanks so the
sentences explain what it shows.**

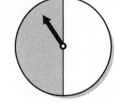

		Second Spin	
		blue	red
First	blue	blue, blue	blue, red
Spin	red	red, blue	red, red

1. If you spin ___blue___ first and ___blue___ second,

   the outcome is ___blue___ , ___blue___ .

2. If you spin ___blue___ first and ___red___ second,

   the outcome is ___blue___ , ___red___ .

3. If you spin ___red___ first and ___blue___ second,

   the outcome is ___red___ , ___blue___ .

4. If you spin ___red___ first and ___red___ second,

   the outcome is ___red___ , ___red___ .

Copyright © Houghton Mifflin Company. All rights reserved.

Use with text pages 608–610.

Locate Points on a Grid

Read this information.

An **ordered pair** tells the location of a point on a grid.

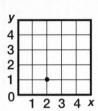

The ordered pair (2, 1) gives the location of this point. To locate this point, do these things.

- Start at 0.

- Move 2 to the right.

- Move 1 up.

Look at the grid below. Notice where the point is. Then use words from the box to fill the blanks.

up	start	right	point

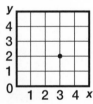

point
Start
right
up

The ordered pair (3, 2) gives the location of this _____. To locate this point, do these things.

- _____ at 0.

- Move 3 to the _____.

- Move 2 _____.

Look at the grid below. Notice where the point is. Then fill in the blanks with the correct numbers.

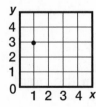

3 The ordered pair (1, __) gives the location of this point. To locate this point, do these things.

- Start at 0.

1 • Move __ to the right.

3 • Move __ up.

Copyright © Houghton Mifflin Company. All rights reserved.   **Use with text pages 616–617.**

Graph Ordered Pairs

Read the definitions.

ordered pair	numbers that give the location of a point on a grid
coordinates	the numbers in an ordered pair
plot	to find the location of
horizontal distance	distance moving sideways
vertical distance	distance moving up-and-down
connect	draw a line between

Use words in bold type to complete the sentences.

(1, 2)

1. Larry will ____connect____ points on a grid to make a line graph.

2. This ____ordered pair____ tells where to locate a certain point on a grid.

3. The ____vertical distance____ between the points on this grid is 2.

4. The ____horizontal distance____ from 0 to the point shown on this grid is 3.

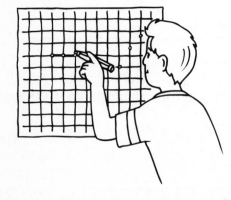

6. The ____coordinates____ of the point shown on this grid are (1, 2).

5. Jorge must ____plot____ the points with the coordinates (0, 4), (1, 4), and (2, 4).

Copyright © Houghton Mifflin Company. All rights reserved.

Use with text pages 618–619.

Name _____   Date _____

Algebra: Graph Functions

**Look at the words and the pictures that show
their meanings.**

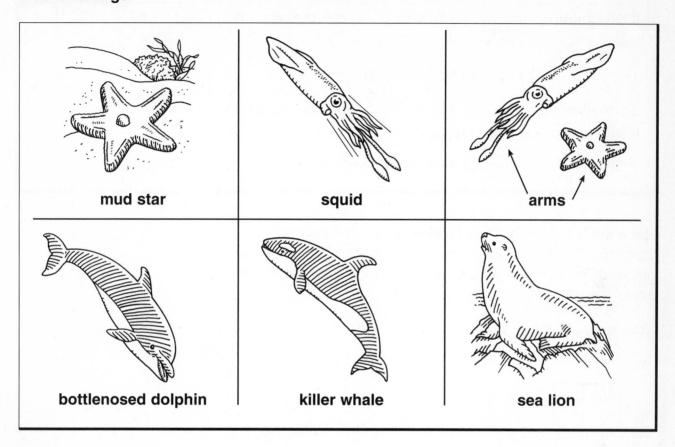

mud star	squid	arms
bottlenosed dolphin	killer whale	sea lion

**Draw lines to connect the words with the descriptions
that tell about them.**

1. mud star

2. squid

3. arms

4. bottlenosed dolphin

5. killer whale

6. sea lion

This huge creature likes to lie on rocks
near the sea.

This long-armed creature swims and floats
in the sea.

This mammal lives in the sea and looks like
it is smiling.

These extend out from the body.

This long-armed creature lives on the
sea floor.

This sea mammal is large, but others with
the same name are larger.

Copyright © Houghton Mifflin Company. All rights reserved.

Use with text pages 620–622.

Integers

Read this information.

If you **gain** an amount of something, you can represent it
with a plus sign and an integer.

Darrell earned four dollars. → +4

If you **give up** an amount of something, you can represent
it with a minus sign and an integer.

Lucia spent two dollars. → ⁻2

**Read each sentence. Decide whether the person is
gaining or *giving up* an amount of something. Circle your
answer. Then write a plus or minus sign and an integer to
show the change.**

1. Erlinda found 5 buttons. (gain) give up ___ +5 ___

2. Sal climbed 3 flights of stairs. (gain) give up ___ +3 ___

3. Toby spent 14 dollars. gain (give up) ___ −14 ___

4. Robyn dived down 20 feet. gain (give up) ___ −20 ___

5. Homer picked 6 quarts
   of berries. (gain) give up ___ +6 ___

6. Faye ate 7 spring rolls. gain (give up) ___ −7 ___

7. Homer gave 4 quarts of berries
   to friends. gain (give up) ___ −4 ___

Copyright © Houghton Mifflin Company. All rights reserved.

Use with text pages 624–626.

Name _____ Date _____

Use a Graph

Look at these pictures of activities.

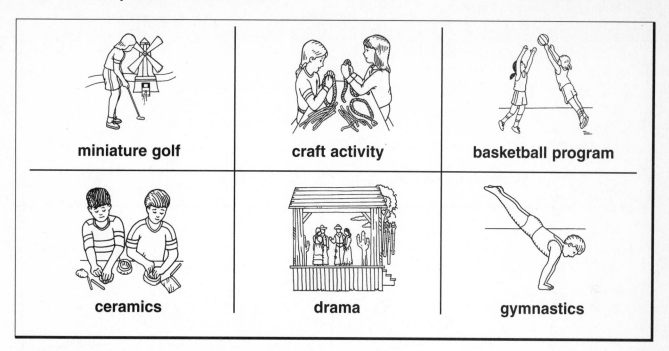

miniature golf	**craft activity**	**basketball program**
ceramics	**drama**	**gymnastics**

**These sentences tell what activities some kids chose at
a recreation center. Write words from the box to complete
the sentences.**

miniature golf	**craft activity**	**basketball program**
ceramics	**drama**	**gymnastics**

1. Claire wants to become an actress. She likes to read plays and act out scenes.
   She signed up for _____. drama

2. Roland likes to use his hands to make things. He wants to make some cups
   for his dad. He signed up for _____. ceramics

3. Lauren likes games of all kinds. She can handle a golf club well. She signed
   up for _____. miniature golf

4. Cosette and Alba like to make things out of paper, string, beads, or cloth.
   They signed up for a _____. craft activity

5. Phil can do many exercises. He can do a headstand and a handstand.
   He signed up for _____. gymnastics

6. Nadine can dribble and shoot a basketball. She wants to learn to pass better.
   She signed up for the _____. basketball program

Copyright © Houghton Mifflin Company. All rights reserved.

Use with text pages 628–630.